FOREWORD AND CONTENTS

The 'Eavy Metal team are Games Workshop's dedicated figure painters, widely regarded as being some of the world's very best miniatures painters. Their beautifully painted miniatures appear in our army books, codexes and every month in the pages of White Dwarf.

'Eavy Metal Masterclasses are amongst the most popular White Dwarf articles, each one showcasing the incredible talents of the painters and the incredible techniques they employ. Each 'Eavy Metal Masterclass lifts the lid on the secrets that go into producing a world-class paintjob, offering an insight into the theory behind each miniature and the techniques and colours employed. But that's not all an 'Eavy Metal Masterclass does, for each article hopefully inspires the reader to pick up their paintbrush and try a new technique out, to have a go at painting something equally spectacular.

Although many people read the 'Eavy Metal Masterclasses and think 'I'm never going to be able to paint that well', with time, patience and practice, anything is possible. It's how many of the 'Eavy Metal team started, after all. And that's why we've collected some of our favourite 'Eavy Metal Masterclasses from past issues of White Dwarf together in a single volume: to showcase some of the best-painted miniatures in the world, to provide great stage-by-stage painting guides and to inspire other painters to 'have a go.'

SUBMISSIONS All material submitted to us for publication is only accepted on the assumption that the copyright in it is, by the very act of submission, unconditionally assigned by the author as beneficial owner and with full title guaranteed to Games Workshop Limited. We also retain the right to edit and/or amend all material as we see fit. So, if you do not wish to assign copyright in this way, please do not send us your submission. We're afraid we cannot work in any other way! Full details of our submissions policy can be found on the legal section of our website at: http://www.games-workshop.com

CORRESPONDENCE We welcome comments about White Dwarf, Games Workshop games and Citadel miniatures. All letters except subscriptions and Mail Order should be addressed to: White Dwarf, Games Workshop, Willow Road, Lenton, Nottingham NG7 2WS.

Please mark your envelope clearly with the name of the game you are writing to us about. If you want a reply you must enclose a self-addressed stamped envelope (overseas readers should include IRCs). We receive an enormous amount of mail. We do read every letter but it may take a little time for us to reply to you, so please be patient!

You can find Games Workshop online at the following address:

www.games-workshop.com

ASK 'EAVY METAL

The world's best miniature painters are always ready to answer your queries. If you have a question or problem that needs solving then write to 'Eavy Metal at the address below – we'll print the best in White Dwarf.

White Dwarf,
Games Workshop,
Design Studio,
Willow Road, Lenton,
Nottingham,
NG7 2WS
United Kingdom

CAPTAIN SICARIUS

WARHAMMER
40,000

For the first of our Masterclasses we turn to 'Eavy Metal's Joe Tomaszewski, who unleashes his incredible talents upon the formidable (and highly detailed) Captain Sicarius.

Cato Sicarius is amongst the greatest heroes of the Ultramarines. His titles are many: Captain of the 2nd Company, Master of the Watch, Knight Champion of Macragge, Grand Duke of Talassar and High Suzerain of Ultramar. Each reflects but a fraction of a lifetime's diligent and exceptional service.

At his heart, Sicarius is an exemplary warrior, a superb swordsman and a formidable shot. He fights with all the passion and zeal of his forebears, his skill at arms a fitting homage to the ancient Primarch of his Chapter, Roboute Guilliman. Armed with a Talassarian tempest blade, Sicarius carves his ways through the ranks of the foe, every blow he delivers leaves a mortal wound, his mighty frame punching his ornate power sword through armour, flesh and bone with ease.

Was Captain Sicarius known only for his skill in combat, he would doubtless own a great legend, but his tactical accumen is perhaps his greatest weapon. Sicarius has taken the famed Space Marine preference for lightning assault to a higher level, delivering punishing attacks against the foe without a moment's notice.

As the tales of his triumphs grow ever longer, Sicarius' name has become a byword for victory. He is a legend formed in the brutal maelstrom of battle, known to all, even beyond the borders of Ultramar.

For such a legendary character an equally impressive miniature was needed, and sculptor Dave Thomas obliged with a great-looking figure that was ripe for the 'Eavy Metal Masterclass treatment.

The talented Joe Tomaszewski was tasked with the paint job and he immediately set to work first by cleaning up all the metal components, removing the flash and mould lines. Joe then decided on his head and weapon options, going with the helmeted head and plasma pistol before undercoating with Chaos Black.

Sicarius' gauntlets and backpack, even though they're not currently attached to the main model, were painted using the same blue technique as described in the box below. Joe checked how these components would appear in their final position when attached to the model, so that the highlights looked as though they were coming from the same light source.

Sicarius has a very 'closed' posture, meaning that if you assemble the entire model you'll make it virtually impossibly to access all the detail with your brush.

Bearing this in mind, Joe attached the head, as that wouldn't form an obstacle. The backpack and both the hands were kept off the model, as they would have prevented Joe from getting to the torso and cloak.

When working on a model like this it's always best to paint the obstructing components before attaching them to the model. In most cases it's obvious what items will hinder painting, but if you're unsure you can simply do a 'test fit' by sticking all the components together temporarily with adhesive putty, and checking what parts of the model you can and can't get at with your brush.

Painting Blue

Step 1. *Joe began by basecoating the power armour with Regal Blue. He did this using several thin layers rather than one thick coat.*

Step 2. *A shade using a 1:1 mix of regal Blue and Chaos Black, was then applied to the recesses of the power armour.*

Step 3. *Joe then started on the highlights, first by applying a 1:1 mix of Ultramarines Blue and Regal Blue to the edges and ridges of the armour.*

Step 4. *Pure Ultramarines Blue was applied next, working up the highlight started in the previous step, on the edges of the power armour.*

Step 5. *The next highlight was a 1:1 mix of Ultramarines Blue and Space Wolves Grey. The highlight stages were also applied to other raised details on the armour, such as the studs.*

Step 6. *A final, fine highlight of pure Space Wolves Grey was used on the very edge of the worked up armour.*

For the silver on Sicarius' weapons and other parts of the model, Joe started with a basecoat of Boltgun Metal. This was then covered with watered-down Chaos Black and, when dry, Joe worked the silver up with Chainmail, before applying a final highlight of Mithril Silver.

Painting a good-looking and realistic gold effect can be quite challenging. The secret to Joe's gold is to get a good basecoat coverage. He achieves this by always using a Scorched Brown and Shining Gold mix for his basecoat.

The other issue is that metallic paints are, by their very nature, a thick consistency, which can lead to a gloopy effect if applied straight from the pot. To combat this Joe always applies his metallics in very thin layers. Thinning down metallic paint can lead to it separating, so make sure you mix in the water vigorously before you apply it to your subject. Also, don't be frightened to highlight your gold with Mithril Silver for that super-polished effect.

Painting Gold

Step 1. For the gold areas Joe started with a basecoat mixed from equal parts Shining Gold and Scorched Brown.

Step 2. A few thin layers of pure Shining Gold were then applied to all but the most recessed parts of the decoration.

Step 3. Joe worked the gold area up over several layers by blending the Shining Gold with Mithril Silver until he was working with a 1:1 mix of both colours.

Step 4. After blending, Joe went back to shading. Using a 1:1 mix of Scorched Brown and Chaos Black, he carefully darkened the deepest recesses of the gold areas.

Step 5. For the last, hard highlight, pure Mithril Silver was used on the edges of the most prominent raised areas.

Step 6. Finally, Joe used both purple and green glazes – watered down Citadel Washes – on different parts of the gold, to slightly change the look and add an extra nuance to the model.

Painting the Cloak

As you can see, Joe's come up with something really special by painting a superb freehand design that follows the contours of the cloak, clarifying why this is an 'Eavy Metal Masterclass rather than a mere Painting Workshop!

Before you start something as ambitious as a complicated freehand pattern, sketch it out on paper first so you know what you're painting. Once you're happy with the pattern, paint it onto the model, being as neat as you can with as steady a hand as possible. Don't worry about getting it completely right first time, if you make a mistake you can always paint over it and try again. Joe had to do this more than once – you'll need a lot of time and patience. When you have the pattern down, the secret to good freehand design is the time spent sharpening up the image, using both the background and foreground colour to get the edges as defined as possible.

Painting the Outside

Step 1. The outside of the cloak was first painted with a basecoat of Scab Red.

Step 2. The cloak was then carefully shaded using watered-down Chaos Black.

Step 3. Joe then carefully blended the folds of the cloak back up to Scab Red.

Step 4. Joe painted Red Gore in thin layers onto the prominent ridges of the cloak.

Step 5. He then highlighted further using a 1:1 mix of Red Gore and Blood Red.

Step 6. For the sharpest highlight, Vomit Brown and Skull White were added to the previous mix.

Painting the Lining

Step 1. The basecoat was painted using a 1:1 mix of Regal Blue and Charadon Granite. He kept this in a pot as he needed it for later.

Step 2. The cloak was highlighted using the existing mix with half as much Bleached Bone added.

Step 3. Joe blended the cloak outwards, using the previous mix but adding more Bleached Bone for every thin layer applied, and then going up to Skull White.

Step 4. Joe then painted on his initial design using thinned-down Bleached Bone.

Step 5. Next, he began sharpening up and clarifying the design using Bleached Bone and the previous Charadon Granite mix.

Step 6. The design was highlighted in exactly the same places as the cloak lining with Skull White and shaded using the previous mix.

The blue on the banner was painted on using the same method as described for the power armour. The red was built up using the same technique as the back of the cloak, but without the black wash.

When painting sculpted back banners, the same general principals apply as to painting a model. However, with a miniature you'll usually paint from the inside out so any excess splashes you make will be covered over in later stages. With a back banner you should paint from the rearmost layer working towards the front for the same reasons.

A feature on Sicarius' banner is the aquila in the centre. Joe has painted it to look like gold but because it's meant to be on a cloth banner he hasn't used metallics. Instead, Joe has used muted browns and yellows that are not as extreme as a 'non-metallic metal' effect, but still get the look of faux tapestry gold rather than real metallic gold.

Painting Cream

Step 1. Joe started with a basecoat of Charadon Granite, liberally coating the whole area including the entire back of the banner.

Step 2. Next, he painted the raised areas using a 1:1 mix of Charadon Granite and Bleached Bone.

Step 3. Joe began to add increasing amounts of Bleached Bone to the previous mix, blending each thin, layered highlight up to pure Bleached Bone.

Step 4. From Bleached Bone, Joe blended up to Skull White, again using many thin layers rather than two separate coats.

Painting a Gold Effect

Step 1. For the faux gold effect, Joe applied a 1:1 mixture of Snakebite Leather and Chaos Black as a basecoat.

Step 2. Pure Snakebite Leather was then applied onto the area as a mid-tone.

Step 3. A highlight using a 1:1 mix of Snakebite Leather and Skull White was then used where the banner creases. No paint was applied to the shaded recess.

Step 4. Skull White was applied for a final, harsh highlight; again, the shade created by the folds of the cloth was ignored for this step.

The white plate on the shoulder, and the white Chapter badge on the cloak clasp, were given a basecoat of Codex Grey, then a layer of Fortress Grey, followed by several thin coats of Skull White.

All of the gems were painted with a 1:1 mix of Blood Red and Chaos Black. Blood Red was applied to the bottom, followed by a crescent of Blazing Orange. A highlight using a 1:1 mix of Sunburst Yellow and Skull White was added to the bottom half, while a dot of Skull White was added to the top. The gems were finished with Gloss Varnish.

The whole plume was first painted Codex Grey, then highlighted with Fortress Grey and Skull White. The red sections were picked out and painted using the same technique as used on the cloak. Joe separated the two areas with a thin black line. When painting plumes, always apply the paint in outwards strokes to follow the detail.

This freehand Crux Terminatus was painted with Fortress Grey and then highlighted with Skull White. Regal Blue and Skull White were used to tidy and define the design.

Not only did Joe paint a complicated pattern in freehand, but the design stretches and warps, following the contours of the flowing cloak.

SKULLTAKER

ject for this
etal Painting
lass is the
s Herald of
Skulltaker, a
Bloodletter.
aszewski takes
infamous
of Khorne.

Skulltaker, Bloodletter and chosen champion of Khorne, is a name feared across the corpse-strewn battlefields of the Warhammer world and the blasted warzones of the 41st Millennium.

Skulltaker bears many monikers, but all tell of his atavistic fury when confronted by enemy warriors. As Khorne's immortal champion it is his duty to meet the greatest heroes of the enemy and destroy them utterly, proving the undeniable might of the Blood God for all to see. As such, Skulltaker does not just defeat his foes, but crush them utterly. He fights with such speed that his glittering black blade is a blur, smashing limbs until Skulltaker's victim can no longer fight. Then, with murderous glee, he claims the fallen hero's skull as a prize for his master.

Wherever the red-skinned Daemon treads, death and destruction surely follow, as Skulltaker seeks to add another polished skull to the vast pile upon the parapet of Khorne's brass citadel. So great is this fearful devotion to the Blood God that all who approach his lair can see it – a soaring mound of polished skulls, black eyes staring lifeless into the blood red skies. The skulls of those of the enemy who prove the greatest challenge, Skulltaker keeps for himself, a rare privilege amongst Khorne's servants. These he hangs upon the hooks that adorn his dark cloak, each a testament to a hard-won duel or a bloody battle that brought delight to his master.

The fearsome Skulltaker model was sculpted by the talented Citadel miniatures designer Mark Harrison. The miniature depicts Khorne's champion on foot, swathed in the skulls from which he takes his name. He is posed with his sword slicing forwards, brandishing the newly harvested skull of a defeated foe at his enemies, wreathed in infernal fire.

For this 'Eavy Metal Masterclass, we gave the job of bringing Khorne's Herald to life to Joe Tomasewski.

The first step for Joe was to clean up the miniature, removing any flash or mould lines with a hobby knife and files. Next, he had to assemble the figure and undercoat it with Chaos Black Spray.

Throughout the painting process, Joe kept Skulltaker's head separate from the rest of the body, mounting it on a flying stand for ease of painting.

This close-up of Skulltaker's hand shows the superb 'Eavy Metal-standard blending techniques that Joe used to paint the skin.

Joe painted Skulltaker in two separate parts, painting the head and body separately so as to be able to paint the detail on the chest and the back of the head properly. He started by painting Skulltaker from the inside out, starting with the red skin. The basecoat for the skin was made up of a series of thin layers of Scab Red, applied directly over the Chaos Black undercoat, followed by successively brighter shades. Throughout the painting process, Joe's technique involved using lots of thin layers of paint, building them up to blocks of solid colour. This allows for a smooth effect between the highlights, creating a subtle gradation of colour across the whole surface.

Painting the red skin

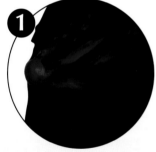

Step 1. Lots of thin layers of Scab Red were painted over the Chaos Black undercoat, to form the basecoat. The thin coats built up to form a solid colour, producing a very smooth effect.

Step 2. The next step was to paint a mix of 1:1 Blood Red and Red Gore over the basecoat, once again using lots of thin layers to build up a subtle highlight.

Step 3. The next layer was a highlight of 1:1 Blood Red and Blazing Orange, applied to the raised areas of the skin and blended into the previous coat.

Step 4. Joe applied a 1:1 mix of Chaos Black and Scorched Brown to the recesses of the skin as a shade. Finally, he applied a 1:1 mix of Blazing Orange and Iyanden Darksun as a highlight to the uppermost areas of the skin.

Eyes and Teeth

Joe painted the eyes and teeth early on in the painting process, at the same time as the skin. The eyes were painted Blazing Orange and then highlighted with Sunburst Yellow and Skull White. The teeth were painted Charadon Granite and were highlighted with Bleached Bone.

After the skin, Joe focused his attention on Skulltaker's flowing cloak, lavishing particular attention to the ornate symbol of Khorne emblazened on its lining. The cloak was painted in such a way that the material resembled shiny black leather, no doubt made from the flayed hides of previous victims.

The leather effect was kept deliberately subtle, to emphasise the most eye-catching area of the cloak – the large symbol of Khorne. Joe painted the cloak using a non-metallic metal effect to make it look like it was still a part of the fabric of the cloak, but still presented in a distinctive Khornate brass colour.

Cloak Fabric

Joe painted the material of the cloak to look as though it is made from leather. He painted a 1:1 basecoat of Chaos Black and Codex Grey over the cloak, leaving Chaos Black in the recesses. Successive highlights of Codex Grey, and Fortress Grey were then painted to the raised areas. Finally a fine line of Skull White was painted along the uppermost areas of the cloak, giving it that shiny, leather effect.

Painting the Cloak Detail

Step 1. *The detail of the Khorne symbol and the border of the cloak was painted with a basecoat of Scorched Brown, directly over the undercoat.*

Step 2. *The next layer was a highlight of Vermin Brown, applied to the raised areas of the symbol and border as well as to the edges, creating a strongly defined outline.*

Step 3. *A highlight of 1:1 mix of Vermin Brown and Skull White was then painted on the edges and uppermost areas of the detail.*

Step 4. *Finally, a pure Skull White highlight was applied to the extreme edges of the symbol, to make it look shiny.*

At the same time as painting the skulls on Skulltaker's cloak, Joe painted the two that adorn his horns, as described below.

There is barely a part of Skulltaker not covered in skulls, including the base of the miniature.

One of the defining features of Skulltaker are, unsurprisingly, the huge amount of skulls he keeps about his person. From the dozens of skulls hanging from his cloak to those adorning his horns, he is practically covered in them, so it would have been remiss of Joe not to lavish particular attention onto them!

The skulls have been painted with a basecoat of Charadon Granite, then highlighted up with increasingly lighter mixes of Bleached Bone and Skull White. Joe used Charadon Granite for the basecoat so as to give the skulls a dirty-grey look, making them appear old and weathered. Once again, Joe applied the colour in many thin layers.

Painting the skulls

Step 1. A pure coat of Charadon Granite was applied as the basecoat, directly over the undercoat, leaving the Chaos Black showing in the recesses, especially in the eye sockets.

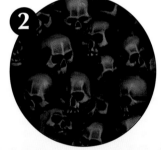

Step 2. The first highlight applied to the skulls was a 1:1 mix of Charadon Granite and Bleached Bone, applied to most of the surface of the skulls.

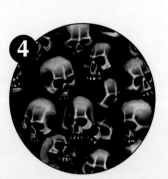

Step 3. The next step was to apply a highlight of pure Bleached Bone to the edges and upper surfaces of the skulls. Note that Joe has left the grey coat showing on part of the skulls, giving them a weathered, dirty look.

Step 4. The final highlight of pure Skull White was applied to the extreme edges and raised surfaces of the skulls, giving the bones a slightly chalky appearance, lending to the aged look Joe was going for.

A top-down view of Skulltaker's horned head, showing the brass skulls that decorate his helmet.

The skulls that make up Skulltaker's cloak, showing the multitude of brass hooks on which they hang. Joe painted the skulls first, before going back to add in the metal detail.

For the final stage, Joe painted all of the metallic areas on Skulltaker, such as the iron armour, the bronze details and symbols adorning the armour, the carved bronze skulls on his helmet, and the countless brass hooks on his cloak. Unlike the symbols painted on his cloak, Joe used metallic paints to get the metal effect.

Joe started by painting the iron areas, as they underlaid all of the bronze details, so Joe could paint them without risk of getting paint on the bronze. Both the iron and the bronze were painted in a similar way, with a metallic and Chaos Black mix for the basecoat, highlighted up to pure metal and then dulled down with Devlan Mud wash.

Painting Iron

Step 1. Joe painted the iron areas of Skulltaker first, basecoating them with a 1:1 mix of Chaos Black and Boltgun Metal.

Step 2. The raised areas of the iron were then highlighted with a coat of pure Chainmail, leaving the basecoat showing in the recesses.

Step 3. The effect of the iron was a little too bright and shiny, so Joe used a wash of Devlan Mud to dull it down, giving it a matt finish.

Step 3. After the wash, a final highlight of Mithril Silver was drybrushed lightly over the top, giving the iron a subtle brightness.

Painting Bronze

Step 1. Joe left the metal details coated in Chaos Black. After the iron had been painted, the bronze was painted with a basecoat of 1:1 Dwarf Bronze and Chaos Black.

Step 2. The metal details were then highlighted with a coat of Dwarf Bronze, leaving the basecoat showing towards the very edges of the symbol.

Step 3. As with the iron areas, the bronze effect was a little bright at this stage. Joe dulled the bronze down a little with a wash of Devlan Mud.

Step 3. For the final stage, the edges and raised surfaces of the bronze were painted with a 1:1 mix of Dwarf Bronze and Mithril Silver, giving it a subtle shine.

A close-up showing the detail Joe has painted on the tongue, using a 1:1 mix of Hormagaunt Purple and Liche Purple, highlighted all the way up to Fortress Grey at the edges of the tongue.

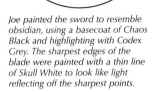

Joe painted the sword to resemble obsidian, using a basecoat of Chaos Black and highlighting with Codex Grey. The sharpest edges of the blade were painted with a thin line of Skull White to look like light reflecting off the sharpest points.

The claws were painted in the same way as the blade of the sword, with lighter strokes of Codex Grey and Skull White painted on to represent growth lines.

The finished sword, showing the obsidian blade and the brass details of the ornate cross-guard.

To finish up, Joe added some fine detailing to the model. He applied finishing touches to Skulltaker's tongue, obsidian blade and his claws. The final detail was the fire wreathed-skull in Skulltaker's hand. Painting realistic-looking fire calls for the reverse of conventional shading and highlighting, starting with the lightest colour – Skull White – in the recesses, and ending up with the darkest, Chaos Black, at the tips, to represent the hottest, brightest area at the heart of the fire.

After finishing, Joe glued the head to the body and based the miniature with sand, painting it with Devlan Mud before drybrushing it Vomit Brown and Bleached Bone.

Painting Fire

Step 1. Unusually, Joe worked backwards from Skull White when painting the fire, working up to 'lowlights' of increasingly darker colours towards the edges.

Step 2. The first step was Sunburst Yellow painted on all of the raised areas, leaving Skull White showing in the recesses to represent the hottest parts of the fire.

Step 3. The next step was Blazing Orange, painted on the flame edges. It is harder to blend darker colours on top of lighter, so Joe used even more layers than usual.

Step 3. The final layer was Scab Red with a highlight of Chaos Black on the flame tips. Skull White specks were painted onto the flames to represent hot cinders.

ORK WARBOSS

WARHAMMER 40,000

Here Darren Latham takes on the plastic Ork Warboss from the Assault on Black Reach boxed game. His brief was to unleash the full power of his painting and kit-bashing skill upon Brian Nelson's iconic plastic Ork.

Warbosses are the mightiest members of Ork society, hulking brutes whose muscular bulk and raw strength makes them natural leaders.

Orks are respecters first and foremost of killiness and kunnin' and those within their number who possess those two virtues in the greatest quantities are destined for greatness. It's all well and good being tough and strong, but if you're not kunnin' and you get ideas above your station you'll find yourself stabbed in the guts by a rival, if you're lucky. If you're not lucky, you'll find yourself the victim of a tellyporta mishap, squig-pen outbreak or worse.

Likewise, there's no point being kunnin'. All Grots are kunnin' but da Boyz don't listen to them and they're no good at krumpin' 'eads. It's far better to be both, if you want to want to rise to the top. To these figures flock Orks by the hundred, the horde increasing until a Waaagh! is launched, a greenskin crusade that will drown worlds in blood and destruction.

As the Citadel design team continue to hone their craft th every new release,

plastic models seem to get better and better. The plastic miniatures of today are highly characterful and detailed models, as much at home as centrepieces in their own right as they are in units. With this in mind, we decided it was high time that the 'Eavy Metal team tackled a plastic miniature for one of our Masterclasses.

The Ork Warboss from the Assault on Black Reach boxed game was the perfect candidate for the job, and Darren Latham, in his first Masterclass, took on the task.

Because plastic is such a versatile material we encouraged Darren to put his conversion skills to the test (with a little help from miniatures designer Seb Perbet). The plastic Ork Nobz kit was perfect for this, and Darren used spare components from it to make a truly unique Warboss.

Before Darren started painting the model he planned out what components to use. Darren wanted to create a Bad Moon Warboss and let that concept guide his component selection. Before sticking bits together he did a 'dry run' with adhesive putty to make sure the conversion worked.

Conversion Bitz

Darren wanted to 'open up' the figure and expose more of the Ork's frontage. To do this he twisted the right arm outward and turned the head more at the neck. This was done by cutting into both the arm and neck joint and forcing the gaps open a little way to widen them. Green Stuff was used to fill the gaps he'd created.

Darren made sure that all the components he used didn't alter the flow and direction of the model. A common mistake in conversions is to have hair flowing one way while a banner is flying in another direction – this can ruin the impact and realism of a miniature.

Darren replaced the original Warboss head with another from the Nobz frame. The jaw plate was added to get an even meaner visage. The topknot was another component from the Nobz Kit. Darren made sure the hair was blowing in the same direction as the other elements of the model.

Every Ork Warboss needs a pet Squig, and one was added to the shoulder of the model for a bit of character. No doubt it's ready to bite the face off any opponent that comes within reach!

The bosspole from the Nobz frame was affixed to the back of the Warboss. The hair tied to the pole is blowing in the same direction as the topknot and loin cloth.

Darren added a buzzsaw to the power klaw first but thought that it unbalanced the model. To rectify this, he made the gun larger with a chain-blade attachment.

The buzzsaw was added as Darren wanted to make the power klaw even bigger and more vicious than it was to start with.

Extra Parts

The frames of our plastic kits, such as the Ork Nobz, are packed with extra bitz and there are more components than you need to assemble the boxed models. As every hobbyist knows, you should never throw these away – add them to your bitz box and save for another project.

The veins were painted in the same manner as the blue under the eyelids. The redness of the skin where the flesh meets the bioniks was painted using the same method as the lips (see below).

Darren paid special attention to the bunched muscles on the arm. These were defined using the method and colours described below, but each stage was built up in a succession of thin layers rather than a single thick coat, for a smooth finish.

You always want your heroes and characters to stand out, especially in an army as infantry heavy as the Orks. While the size and aesthetics of a character model help differentiate between them and your average Ork Boy, 'Eavy Metal use a more subtle technique to further define this for the Orks by adding yellow to the skin colour.

The yellow in the mix lifts the skin tone, making it brighter and stronger so it catches the eye. Another tip for making your model stand out is to always use the same highlight colour. For instance, the lips, blue veins and skin all use Bleached Bone as the basis for the highlight colour, tying the flesh tones together.

Painting the Skin

Step 1. The skin of the Warboss was first given a basecoat of Orkhide Shade. This was followed by a wash using a 1:1 mix of Chaos Black and Badab Black.

Step 2. Darren then built up a layer of Knarloc Green over all of the flesh areas apart from the deeper recesses.

Step 3. Pure Goblin Green was then painted over the previous layer; the recesses and creases in the skin were avoided to let the Knarloc Green show through.

Step 4. Next, a 4:1:1 mix of Goblin Green, Golden Yellow and Bleached Bone was applied to the raised areas.

Step 5. The same mix of colours was used again for this stage, only the proportions were 2:1:1 of Goblin Green, Golden Yellow and Bleached Bone.

Step 6. The flesh was finished off with an extremely thin layer of Bleached Bone, applied carefully to the most prominent areas.

After the skin, Darren tackled the talons, using a 1:1 basecoat mix of Orkhide Shade and Hawk Turquoise. These were highlighted with Rotting Flesh.

The lower eyelids were painted with a 1:1 mix of Regal Blue and Goblin Green. The lips were painted with a 1:1 Scab Red and Goblin Green mix.

Painting the Clothing

Darren imagined the gun holsters as being made from the same material as the Ork's trousers, so they were painted using an identical method to the brown cloth.

The stitching was lined with black to help define the detail. This was done with a Badab Black wash followed by painting in a thin line of Chaos Black.

Darren used Kommando Khaki as the main highlight for both the brown and black cloth. He didn't want to use a traditional highlight colour like grey for the black areas as this would be a very stark highlight, suggesting that the material was made of leather, while Darren wanted it to look more like cloth.

A Kommando Khaki highlight also suggests a cool colour and Darren wanted the cloth to be painted in cooler tones so it would contrast with the warm yellows that he planned to use on the armour. A key aspect of colour theory is recognising warm and cool colours and then using them as contrasts to get a pleasing effect.

Painting the Brown Clothing

Step 1. The cloth was first basecoated with a 1:1 mix of Scorched Brown and Khemri Brown followed by a wash of Badab Black.

Step 2. A 2:2:1 mix of Scorched Brown, Khemri Brown and Kommando Khaki was applied to the raised areas.

Step 3. The same brown mix was used for the next layer, but with more Kommando Khaki added.

Step 4. Pure Kommando Khaki was used as the final highlight, applied to the most pronounced parts of the folds and creases.

Painting the Black Clothing

Step 1. Darren started with a 4:1 basecoat mix of Chaos Black and Kommando Khaki. A wash using watered-down Scorched Brown was then applied.

Step 2. The black was then layered up using a 1:1 mix of Chaos Black and Kommando Khaki.

Step 3. Darren continued to build up the layers. This time he added more Kommando Khaki to the mix, using a 3:1 mix of Kommando Khaki and Chaos Black.

Step 4. As with the areas of brown cloth, the final stage used a coat of pure Kommando Khaki as the final highlight layer.

Painting the Metal

The belt buckle was painted using the dark metal technique, as described below.

The visible parts of the guns poking out from the holsters were also painted using Darren's dark metal technique.

As with many Orks, there's a lot of metal on this model so it's a good idea to paint it in two ways. Darren's gone for dark metal and brass. Not only will these two colours contrast well against each other but the dark metal will get a warm red rust effect and the brass will have a cooler verdigris look painted on. This will bring two further contrasting colours into the mix, helping define the model even further.

For some of the rust effect, Darren used a stippling technique. This involved using an old brush and lightly 'dappling' the paint onto the desired areas. When using this to get a rusty effect, take a 'less is more' approach.

Painting the Brass

Step 1. A 1:1:1 mix of Tin Bitz, Dwarf Bronze and Scorched Brown was used as the basecoat. This was followed by a 1:1 wash of Chaos Black and Badab Black.

Step 2. A mid-tone was then applied using the same basecoat mix with a small amount of Mithril Silver added to it.

Step 3. A thin wash using a 1:1 mix of Dark Angels Green and Hawk Turquoise was then applied to the rivets and recesses.

Step 4. Mithril Silver was used as a final highlight, while just a small dab of Rotting Flesh was added to some of the deeper recesses.

Painting the Dark Metal

Step 1. The silver metal parts were first painted Boltgun Metal. A wash using a 1:1 mix of Chaos Black and Badab Black was then applied.

Step 2. Darren then used a wash of thinned-down Scorched Brown. This was applied directly into the recessed areas.

Step 3. A wash with thinned Bestial Brown, followed by a second wash of Vermin Brown, was painted into the recesses. This was also stippled along the klaw.

Step 4. The metal was then highlighted with Chainmail. Mithril Silver was used sparingly to emphasise the sharpness of the klaw blades.

Painting the Armour

After the armour was painted, Darren added some characteristic Bad Moon details, such as these flames, which were carefully painted on with Chaos Black.

Darren made use of other motifs, such as the chequers on the jaw plate and the dags on the shoulder pad. These were first painted in Chaos Black and then highlighted with Codex Grey.

After painting the yellow armour, Darren added some additional livery in the form of black flames, chequers and dags on the shoulder plates – all classic Ork motifs.

He then came to painting the chips on the armour and for this he wanted to do something different. Rather than simply painting on a scratch in Mithril Silver, he wanted to create a layered effect; some chips have simply uncovered the previous layer of paint, some are so old that rust is now visible, while the more recent chips have revealed the bare metal beneath the primer. Darren achieved this by 'working backwards', painting the chips from the outside, then moving in towards the centre.

Painting the Yellow Armour

Step 1. Darren started painting the Bad Moon's armour by first applying a basecoat of Tausept Ochre.

Step 2. A 1:1 mix of Iyanden Darksun and Golden Yellow was then applied to the raised areas of the armour.

Step 3. To get some definition and shade, thinned-down Dark Flesh was painted into the recesses.

Step 4. A highlight using the mix from Step 2 with equal parts Skull White added was then painted onto the prominent areas.

Step 5. For the most extreme highlights, more Skull White – half as much again – was added to the previous mix.

Painting the Paint Chips

Step 1. For the outside of the chip Darren used a 1:1:1 mix of Iyanden Darksun, Golden Yellow and Skull White. This was carefully applied to the shoulder plate.

Step 2. Dark Flesh was then applied to some of the chips. Darren was careful to leave an outline of the previous mix.

Step 3. Boltgun Metal was applied to the centre of some of the chips. Some of the chips were left at this stage to give the impression that the chips vary in age.

Step 4. Mithril Silver was used on a few chips to represent very recent scratches and damage.

The red of the topknot is used as a spot colour across the model. It was painted Scab Red, then Blood Red, followed by Vomit Brown.

The flames on the loincloth were painted in freehand and use the same yellow mix as the armour, with Vomit Brown used for deep shading.

The Squig was painted in Liche Purple, followed by Hormagaunt Purple and Kommando Khaki.

The Squig's hair was painted a Hawk Turquoise and Regal Blue mix, highlighted with Space Wolves Grey.

The Bad Moon banner top was painted in the same way as the yellow armour.

Spent bullet casings can be made by chopping up small lengths of plastic or brass rod.

'EAVY METAL BAD MOON SHOWCASE

Only the richest and most extravagant of Bad Moons – already the richest of Orks – can afford a suit of mega-armour.

The scraps of cloth on this Grot have been painted yellow, marking him out as belonging to the Bad Moon clan.

This Nob has been painted in a similar way to the Warboss, using the same weathering technique on his armour.

Detail of a deathspitter

*Tactical Marines from the Eagle Warriors Chapter (left)
and the Emperor's Eagles Chapter (right).*

Tyranid Hive Tyrant

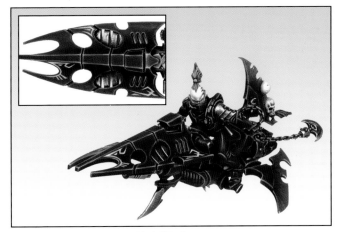

Dark Eldar Reaver

Ork Nobz armed with big choppa (left) and kombi-weapon (right)

Ulthwé Eldar Farseer

CHAOS LORD

Keith Robertson meets the challenge of tackling a towering Chaos Lord in this Masterclass. Here he demonstrates how to tackle a larger, multi-part model, including painting many of the parts separately.

There are few things more terrifying to face in battle than a Chaos Lord, mounted upon a snorting Chaos Steed and armoured for war. Such individuals tower above even other Champions of Chaos, for they are the greatest of the Dark Gods' mortal champions. Swollen with power and possessed of a fearsome skill earned from numberless battles, Chaos Lords are amongst the most deadly of warriors to be found upon the Warhammer world. Any foe brave or foolish enough to face them appear as feeble or fumbling in their shadow. The Champions of Men seem as weakling children, while hulking Orcs appear lumbering and slow, even the greatest of Elves seem frail and weak, despite their haughtiness. When presented with the murderous glory of a Chaos Lord, entire regiments of warriors quail, for they know that they face death incarnate.

These vicious killers lead from the front of their armies, often atop a monstrous creature such as a nightmarish steed or a daemonic creature. Although they will butcher any foe with practiced skill, Chaos Lords, as all champions of the Dark Gods, are especially eager to engage the heroes and commanders of the enemy force, cutting them down without mercy. The foul patrons of the Northmen look admiringly upon such actions, for it is fitting that their chosen warriors should lay low the champions of other, lesser gods.

With such tremendous brutality to live up to, a Chaos Lord should always be an imposing presence on the tabletop with a suitably impressive model to boot. Unsurprisingly, our miniatures designers have stepped up to the mark and provided us with some great models over the years.

For this Masterclass we chose ace sculptor Michael Anderson's brooding Chaos Lord on a Daemonic Steed. The pose of this model oozes menace and makes for a superb army centrepiece. 'Eavy Metal's Keith Robertson stepped foward to meet the challenge of painting this model, in his first 'Eavy Metal Masterclass, eager to show his mettle! Keith started by cleaning the components up and undercoating them Chaos Black.

Painting the Chaos Steed

Keith has chosen to paint the Chaos Lord as a follower of Nurgle and so plans to use drab greens and dull metals to give a suitably decayed appearance. When using such a colour palette it's important to add a contrasting colour. For this model, Keith is using the seared, exposed flesh on the mount to get a rich red which will contrast well against the green of the Lord's armour and the mount's barding.

While working on the skin he also added little nicks and cuts as paint effects to suggest that the steed is as much of a battle-hardened veteran as its rider. These were carefully applied with Keith's steady hand using the Vomit Brown mix used for the steed's skin (see Step 5, below) and then shaded with a 1:1 mixture of Scorched Brown and Chaos Black.

Painting the Steed's Skin

Step 1. Keith started by giving the skin a liberal basecoat of Scorched Brown, making sure he covered the whole area evenly.

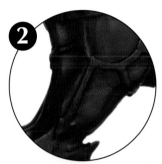

Step 2. He then gave the skin a wash, using a 1:1 mix of Badab Black and Ogryn Flesh, making sure it ran into the recesses.

Step 3. A 1:1 mix of Scorched Brown and Dark Flesh was used as a mid-tone, keeping the darker colours showing in the more recessed areas of the mount's flesh.

Step 4. Keith kept gradating towards the raised areas, this time by adding Scab Red to the previous mix by a 1:2 ratio (one part Scab Red to two parts Step 3 mix).

Step 5. The skin was highlighted by picking out the raised muscle sinews. For this he used Vomit Brown added to the previous mix by 2:1 (two parts Vomit Brown to one part Step 4 mix).

Step 6. A final highlight was used on the sinews using a 1:1 mix of Vomit Brown and the existing highlight mix created in Step 5.

Painting the Branding

Step 1. The mount's Chaos brand was first given a basecoat of Scab Red.

Step 2. For the next stage, Keith applied a 1:2 mix of Scorched Brown and Vomit Brown.

Step 3. Bleached Bone was then added to the brown mix from the previous stage and used to highlight the branding.

Step 1. The barding was first given a basecoat with a 1:2 mix of Chaos Black and Catachan Green.

On first look you may think that the mount's barding and Chaos Lord's armour have been painted using the same colours and technique. But, while they look similar, the rider is actually painted in lighter tones.

Keith's done this so that the eye is drawn to the rider first. This is a useful tip that can be used for any mounted character; painting the rider in lighter colours helps define him whilst keeping the model a cohesive whole.

Step 2. Keith then applied Catachan Green to all but the most recessed areas of the barding.

Painting Chaos Armour

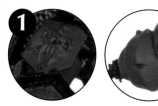

Step 1. The armour was given a basecoat using a 1:1 mix of Knarloc Green and Orkhide Shade, applying it to all but the splayed rims of the poleyn (the knee guard).

Step 2. Pure Knarloc Green was then applied all over the armour, apart from the deepest recesses and around the joints.

Step 3. A 1:2 mix of Rotting Flesh and Catachan Green was then carefully applied to the outer and inner edges of the armour.

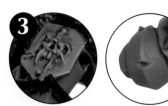

Step 3. Next, Keith mixed Knarloc Green with Desert Yellow using a 1:3 ratio, and applied this to the raised areas and edges of the armour.

Step 4. Keith then added Rotting Flesh to the previous mix in a 1:1 ratio. Again, this was applied to the raised areas for a harsh highlight.

Step 4. A final highlight of Rotting Flesh was applied. Keith then added glazes and damage using the same techniques from the armour (Steps 5 and 6).

Step 5. Several glazes were applied in patches across the armour, concentrating on the shaded areas. Keith used Leviathan Purple, a 6:1 mix of Gryphonne Sepia and Golden Yellow, and a 2:4:1 mix of Baal Red, Ogryn Flesh and Scab Red.

Step 6. A final, fine highlight of Rotting Flesh was also applied. To finish, the armour was given some kinks and cuts of battle damage using the mix from Step 4, which was then carefully shaded with Scorched Brown.

One of the key effects used by Keith is the verdigris'd brass. Verdigris is caused by oxidation of copper or brass, in exactly the same way as rust on iron and steel. Before painting this effect on your model it's best to do a little research. Keith found plenty of useful pictures on the internet; the best ones were of bronze statues found in places such as town squares, where the statue has spent many years exposed to the elements. From these images Keith found that the verdigis is most prominent where water has pooled or dripped into a sculpture's recesses. He has included the drip effect on both the helmet and shield, which really adds to the corroded and decayed look ideal for a Nurgle follower.

Keith has added additional weathering to the model by applying glazes on the armour. He applied these to precise areas, such as under the vambrace and to the recessed areas of the barding, to reinforce the tarnished appearance of the metal.

Shield Close-up

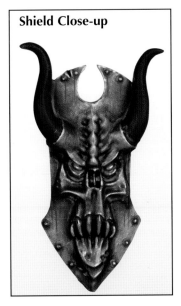

Painting Brass

Step 1. *Keith started with a basecoat using a 1:3 mix of Tin Bitz and Dwarf Bronze.*

Step 2. *Pure Dwarf Bronze was then applied to all but the most recessed areas of the helm.*

Step 3. *A 1:2 mix of Dwarf Bronze and Mithril Silver was used to highlight the raised areas.*

Step 4. *Keith washed the entire helmet with Devlan Mud and then applied a further wash of Badab Black to the recesses.*

Step 5. *For the verdigris, Keith used a thin, 8:1:1 mix of Hawk Turquoise, Orkhide Shade and Skull White.*

Step 6. *A final highlight of Mithril Silver was painted along the edges of the helmet.*

Painting Steel

Step 1. *The Chaos Lord's warhammer was first given a basecoat of Boltgun Metal.*

Step 2. *A Badab Black wash was then applied. Keith kept adding additional wash layers to get a very patchy, blackened look.*

Step 3. *He then added a number of glazes to weather it further, using Hawk Turquoise, Catachan Green and Vermin Brown.*

Step 4. *Finally, Chainmail highlights were applied along the edges of the hammer.*

You may have noticed that Keith uses a lot of glazes when painting, so it's worth explaining exactly what they are and when best to use them. A glaze is very similar to a wash and is made from watered-down paint. The key difference between a wash and glaze is that a wash is used to create shading and depth, while a glaze is used in a series of thin layers to modify and strengthen colours, adding a shine and intensity to particular areas.

Creating a glaze is relatively simple as all you need to do is thin your chosen colour down with lots of water, to the point where you can hardly tell there's any pigment in at all. Keith likes to speed up the process by adding an artists' glaze medium instead of water. When Keith applies a glaze he does it over several thin layers, making sure the previous coat is dry before applying the next. Again, this differs from washes that can be liberally applied in one go.

Painting the Cloak

Step 1. Keith started by giving the cloak a basecoat using a 1:2:2 mix of Chaos Black, Scab Red and Warlock Purple.

Step 2. Keith applied a wash into the recesses using a 4:1 mix of Badab Black and Chaos Black.

Step 3. For the mid-tone he used the Step 1 mix and added Kommando Khaki to it using a 3:1 ratio (three parts Kommando Khaki to one part basecoat mix).

Step 4. Pure Kommando Khaki was used as the final highlight, applied to the most prominent raised areas.

Painting Wood

Step 1. The wood on the underside of the shield was painted with a 1:2 mix of Scorched Brown and Khemri Brown.

Step 2. For the wash, Keith applied two coats of Badab Black, making sure the first coat was dry before applying the second.

Step 3. Keith began highlighting the wood grain with a coat of pure Khemri Brown.

Step 4. For the final highlight, a 1:2 mix of Khemri Brown and Dheneb Stone was applied to the edges and wood grain.

Painting Fur

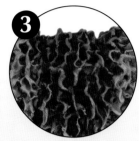

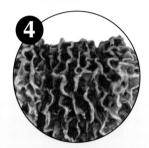

Step 1. The fur was first given an even basecoat using a 1:1 mix of Astronomican Grey and Catachan Green.

Step 2. A wash of Badab Black was then applied. Keith applied several additional layers in a V-shape down the centre of the cloak.

Step 3. A light drybrush of Rotting Flesh was applied all over the cloak, concentrating on the areas either side of the V-shape.

Step 4. Skull White was used as a final highlight; this was more heavily applied towards the edges of the cloak.

Painting Leather

Step 1. The leather straps were simply given an initial coat of Chaos Black. Keith was careful not to drip paint onto the horse's skin.

Step 2. Keith highlighted the leather using a 1:3 mix of Chaos Black and Rotting Flesh. This was applied to the edging and nicks in the leather.

Step 3. For the final highlight, more Rotting Flesh was added to the previous mix using a 1:1 ratio.

Painting Tentacles

Step 1. The Chaos Lord's tentacled left arm was first given a basecoat of pure Tallarn Flesh.

Step 2. Keith added highlights with a 1:2 mix of Tallarn Flesh and Rotting Flesh.

Step 3. More Rotting Flesh was added to the previous mix using a 2:1 ratio (two parts Rotting Flesh to one part mix).

Step 4. A glaze using a 1:1 mix of Liche Purple and Scab Red was then worked into the recesses.

Step 5. An additional glaze, this time using a 2:1 mix of Liche Purple and Regal Blue, followed.

Step 6. Finally, Keith highlighted the tentacled mass with pure Skull White, applying it to the prominent points.

Painted horns can look very intricate but, as with everything in miniature painting, it just takes a bit of practise.

It's all about brush control and letting the bristles do the work. Where you have the light and dark colours meeting, start the brush at the thinnest point and draw it down (or up) the model in gentle strokes, lightly pulling away from the figure. Don't hold the brush like a pencil – rather than holding the brush at a constant level, pulling the brush up towards you changes the way paint flows onto a model.

Painting the Helmet Horns

Step 1. The horns were given a coat of Chaos Black to prime them.

Step 2. Keith then applied a coat of Scorched Brown, covering all but the base of the horn.

Step 3. Calthan Brown was then overlaid in an elongated, jagged pattern, using the brush action described above.

Step 4. Tausept Ochre was then applied in the same manner as the previous step, but not as close to the horn's base.

Step 5. Keith used Bleached Bone for the next layer, staying much closer to the top of the horn.

Step 6. Finally, Skull White was used as a highlight, only applied to the very tips of the horn.

Painting the Mount's Horns

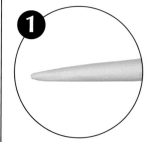

Step 1. The horns on the barding went from light at the base to dark on the tips, so Keith started with a Bleached Bone basecoat.

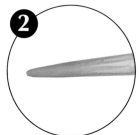

Step 2. Tausept Ochre was painted over the basecoat, creating the elongated jagged pattern similar to the helmet horns.

Step 3. Keith then overlaid the top of the horn with Calthan Brown, not going as close to the base as in the previous stage.

Step 4. Scorched Brown was applied to the top part of the horn, making sure the previous layers were visible towards the base.

Step 5. Chaos Black was applied to the very tip to create the dark-to-light gradating effect.

Step 6. To finish, Keith used Skull White to highlight the very tip and produce a shiny effect.

The saddle was painted using the same technique as used for the leather straps, described earlier.

The hands dangling from the harness were painted with Tallarn Flesh and then highlighted up with a mix of Tallarn Flesh and Catachan Green. They were given a wash of Leviathan Purple and watered-down Catachan Green.

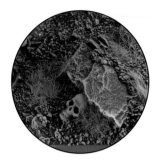

Bases can really enhance a model and Keith has created a gorgeous base for his Chaos Lord. Keith added slate, skulls left over from a Chaos Warriors sprue, and static grass to create an almost dioramic base for his Chaos Lord.

The tail was basecoated with Chaos Black and then highlighted with Hawk Turquoise and Rotting Flesh. The Hawk Turquoise was used because it is a spot colour – with the helmet, the shield, chamfron and the tail all including the colour, it balances out the entire model.

The chainmail was painted using the same metal technique as for the warhammer. To create a contrast, Keith has applied a rust effect where it meets the green horse barding. At the other end of the armour, he's added green to contrast with the red in the mount's ruddy flesh.

The belt buckle was simply basecoated with Boltgun Metal followed by a Chainmail highlight. Keith added the rust effect – using very watered-down Vermin Brown – between the buckle and green armour to create a contrast.

The skulls were deliberately kept a neutral tone, and so were painted with a Scorched Brown and Khemri Brown mix, followed by a Devlan Mud wash and then a highlight of Kommando Khaki.

SPACE WOLVES

WARHAMMER
40,000

Next, Neil Green tackles this fearsome Wolf Guard model, complete with fiery red hair, furry pelts and a pair of wolf claws sheathed in a cool energy field.

WOLF GUARD

The Wolf Guard are the hand-picked Battle-Brothers that form the personal retinue of a Wolf Lord. Every Space Wolves warrior desires a place in the Wolf Guard and will battle even harder when a Wolf Lord is nearby in the hope that he may earn the right to join this legendary brotherhood. Elevation to the ranks of the Wolf Guard brings not only prestige and access to the finest weapons and wargear but also the chance to earn the greatest glory. The Wolf Guard will fight loyally at the side of their lord, cutting down the enemy and committing acts worth of the greatest sagas.

The Wolf Guard don't just act as the Wolf Lord's retinue, however – it is also their duty to accompany packs throughout the force, lending them their wisdom and skill in the heat of battle. Such a duty is considered a great honour, for the Wolf Guard are the elite of the Space Wolves Chapter and thus they owe it to their Battle-Brothers to share their courage and

experience in battle. Thus will a hot-blooded pack of Blood Claws, eager to prove their worth benefit from the battle wisdom and tactical acumen of a Wolf Guard. Likewise the old, set in their ways Long Fangs, whose numbers have been worn down by decades of battle, gain a skilled and experienced addition, lending his might to their formidable firepower.

Juan Diaz sculpted this excellent Wolf Guard model, armed with a pair of wolf claws. The dynamic pose of the model makes him look particularly eager to get in close to the enemy, pouncing forwards with his teeth bared, letting out a battle howl of pure rage.

Neil Green was keen to get his paws on this characterful model. He started by cleaning up the components, carefully, removing any bits of flash, especially from the armour and the claws. The arms were then glued into place, but the backpack was kept separate for now. The model was undercoated Chaos Black.

It is the face of a miniature that draws the eye to it and so some attention needs to be spent on and around it, especially on a model such as this one. Neil has painted the Wolf Guard's face in lighter tones, as this helps the eye immediately define the focal point.

When painting a face with such a strong expression, it's important to keep your paint thin so that you don't lose the detail, so it's best to use two or three thin layers for each stage. If the paint is too thick you not only risk obscuring the detail, but also adding in visible brushstrokes that will detract from the finished effect.

The other point to note is how the hair meets the face. A faint line separates the two areas; again this helps the eye define the focal point of the miniature. When Neil applied the basecoat layer to the face he painted right up to the hair, but with the subsequent stages he didn't work the paint up to the edge, thereby creating a thin boundary line of darker paint.

The teeth were painted Bleached Bone. Neil left the eyes black and then filled in the white of the eye with Bleached Bone, leaving a gap in the middle to create the pupil – steady hands are needed here!

The Face

Step 1. The face was basecoated with a 1:1 mix of Vermin Brown and Scorched Brown.

Step 2. Next, a 2:1:1 mix of Dwarf Flesh, Vermin Brown and Scorched Brown was used. This was applied to all but the recessed areas.

Step 3. Pure Dwarf Flesh was then applied, brushed onto the face as a mid-tone – once again it was left out of the recessed areas.

Step 4. The face was then highlighted, first with a 1:1 mix of Dwarf Flesh and Skull White, applied to the raised areas.

Step 5. A 3:1 mix of Skull White and Bleached Bone was then applied, followed by a 1:1 wash of Gryphonne Sepia and Ogryn Flesh.

Step 6. The eyes and teeth were painted with Bleached Bone, while the highlight was retouched using the mix from Step 5.

The Hair

Step 1. The hair was first painted with Bestial Brown followed by a layer of Blazing Orange.

Step 2. The hair was then given two consecutive washes of Ogryn Flesh, followed by a highlight of Dwarf Flesh applied to each hair strand.

Step 3. Bleached Bone was then applied as a final highlight. To finish, a glaze of Baal Red was brushed over the whole area.

Much of the power armour is obscured by details such as the pelt – it's much more prominent on the rear of the model.

The main part of the backpack was painted in the same way as the power armour.

There are a multitude of methods for painting power armour, many of which have been detailed in White Dwarf. The method employed by 'Eavy Metal has evolved over a good few years and is proven to be very effective. You start by building up a flat colour; this is the basecoat, applied over several thin layers until you have a solid, opaque coat. A highlight is then applied to the edges of each segment and a shade in the joints between the sections. The light source is assumed to be coming from directly overhead, and so the top edges have a more intense highlight. This is best demonstrated on the fist shown in the steps below. You can see in the later stages how the highlight is applied more heavily to the top of the fingers and across the thumb; this lifts the miniature and avoids confusing the eye with multiple light sources.

That's the method in its most general terms but you can add to this with additional paint effects. For instance, we'll be taking a closer look at how to inflict extra battle damage, scratches and chips over the page. Space Wolves power armour is often accented by yellows and reds, as they make good contrasting colours. This is normally applied to the shoulder pads, as we'll cover in more detail later in the article, and it's not unknown for dags or stripes on the arms or legs to be painted onto the armour as well.

The Power Armour

Step 1. *A 1:1:1 basecoat mix of Kommando Khaki, Shadow Grey and Space Wolves Grey was applied to the power armour.*

Step 2. *A 1:1 mix of Shadow Grey and Scorched Brown was carefully brushed into the recesses between the armour sections.*

Step 3. *Next, a 2:1:1 Space Wolves Grey, Shadow Grey and Kommando Khaki was applied towards the edges of the armour.*

Step 4. *Pure Space Wolves Grey was worked onto the edges of the armour, creating a distinct edge highlight.*

Step 5. *Devlan Mud was washed into the recesses between the plates of armour.*

Step 6. *A final highlight using a 1:1 mix of Space Wolves Grey and Skull White was applied, with a stronger application on the top edges.*

The wolf tails get lighter as they taper towards the end, but otherwise use the technique below.

Keeping the backpack separate allows Neil to paint the tails without obstruction.

Painting fur is relatively easy, as the texture is ideal for drybrushing, giving you a pleasing effect with minimal effort. However, this is an 'Eavy Metal-painted model, so it won't surprise you to learn that instead of drybrushing the fur, Neil picked out the separate clumps and highlighted them accordingly. The only exception to this was a very light drybrush in Steps 3 and 4, detailed below.

It's always a good idea to get some real-world reference before you start painting fur. Reference books on natural history are a good starting point, as they often have clear, high-quality photos and, as always, the Internet is a great tool for finding suitable images.

Using real-world reference allows you to paint your fur to look more realistic – for example, the fur on the back of an animal tends to be darker, lightening out towards the underside. Similarly, wolf tails tend to lighten towards the end and so Neil has replicated this effect on the two tails dangling from the backpack. Bleached Bone and Skull White were used more heavily than on the pelts to achieve this lighter tone.

Neil has painted the underside of the pelts red, starting with a basecoat of pure Scab Red. Fortress Grey was added to the mix in gradual stages as he built up the layers until he was happy with the final look.

The Fur

Step 1. The fur areas were first basecoated with Scorched Brown. A solid coat was created using several thin layers.

Step 2. Bestial Brown was then used to pick out the fur, this was more heavily applied towards the edges of the pelt.

Step 3. Vomit Brown was used for the next layer; the centre of the pelt was given a light drybrush, while the fur along the edges was painted.

Step 4. Bleached Bone was lightly drybrushed in the centre of the pelt, but painted onto the clumps of fur around the edges.

Step 5. Skull White was the final highlight, applied over the whole pelt with a slightly heavier coating on the edges.

Step 6. Two washes were then brushed over the pelt; the first was Gryphonne Sepia, followed by Ogryn Flesh when the first wash had dried.

The pair of wolf claws are a real defining feature of the Wolf Guard, and once painted really bring the model together.

Both sides of the wolf claws were painted with the energy effect, as the model's open posture makes every angle visible.

Alternative Style

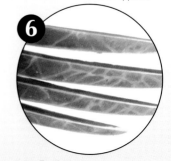

This is an alternative energy field pattern painted on another 'Eavy Metal model – the effect works with a variety of colours.

Neil has painted a brilliant freehand energy field design playing across the wolf claws. You'll see similar effects on many 'Eavy Metal painted models that feature power weapons in one form or another.

Neil started this technique by 'blotching' on the basecoat to the claws. This means the paint, while remaining thinned down, was applied in an almost uncontrolled, roughshod way, letting that paint run onto the area and dry in a natural state rather than being controlled by the brush (see Step 1, below). When dry, this formed the basis of the freehand design. The next stage was to paint on the initial energy lines; these were painted using the pattern created in the previous step as a guide. From there it's a case of building up the freehand work by adding to the energy lines with the subsequent colours and mixes, each stage should have a finer line than the previous one. After each layer, Neil applied an extremely thin glaze of the same colour and washed it over the entire claw. This helps create the 'frosting' effect and adds a certain ethereal quality to the look of the model.

Neil has painted the energy lines in a more tightly packed and denser pattern on the underside of the claws, suggesting the power of the wolf claws is focused on the area of the weapon that will do the most damage.

The Wolf Claws

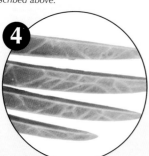

Step 1. Thinned-down Regal Blue was applied to the wolf claws in a haphazard, 'blotchy' fashion, as described above.

Step 2. Lines were painted onto the claws with Hawk Turquoise, using the pattern created in the previous stage as a guide.

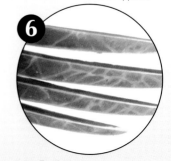

Step 3. A 3:1 mix of Hawk Turquoise and Bleached Bone was painted over the lines. A glaze of the same mix was then applied.

Step 4. A 1:1 mix of Bleached Bone and Hawk Turquoise was used on the lines, then turned into a glaze and brushed over the area.

Step 5. Next, a 3:1 mix of Bleached Bone and Hawk Turquoise was used. Once again this was thinned to a glaze and applied to the whole area.

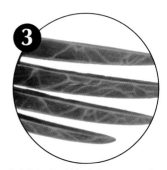

Step 6. Finally, Skull White was painted onto the very edges and points of the claws as an extreme highlight.

BATTLE DAMAGE

Painting battle damage onto power armour can add real character to a model, suggesting these are ancient, well-worn suits of armour, rather than something that's new or mass-produced.

The number of chips, marks or scratches you add is up to you; the more you apply, the more battle-worn the armour will look. Bear in mind that adding too much battle damage can distract from the actual paint scheme. It's also worth thinking about the location of the marks. Most wear and tear will happen around the joints of the armour, but areas such as the greaves and boots will also

see a fair share of scratches and chips from walking amongst the debris of a battlefield. The armour on the arms and fists will often be damaged as well, due to previous close combat encounters.

It's also important to vary the age of the battle damage on the power armour. If every scratch and mark is of the same type, then it will give the impression that all damage has happened in just one battle rather than through the ages. Creating deeper chips suggests older damage, while light scratches or bright silver chips infer more recent incidents.

Step 1. Neil painted on the chips by first reapplying the power armour basecoat – a 1:1:1 mix of Kommando Khaki, Shadow Grey and Space Wolves Grey – in small areas on the armour. For deeper chips the mix was darkened by adding more Shadow Grey.

Step 2. Below the previous application pure Space Wolves Grey was added. Again, the thickness of the line and amount used will depend on the effect you're after, from the size of the chip to the age you want to represent.

Step 3. Skull White was then used underneath the chip, add a small amount just to highlight the damage. You can increase the amount to suggest a more recent chip or scratch.

More Battle Damage Examples

Vehicles such as tanks are often weathered and covered in scratches, especially around areas of heavy use such as ladders, hatches and on 'dozer blades, as in this example.

This White Scars Vanguard Veteran wears an ancient suit of power armour, the age of which is suggested by the heavy chipping.

This Salamanders Dreadnought shows heavy battlefield wear and tear. Severe metallic scratches can be achieved with a basecoat of Boltgun Metal and then a following layer of Mithril Silver. A wash of Badab Black makes the chip look older.

With the main areas of the miniature now painted, Neil started work on the additional details, such as the shoulder pads, gems and runes. Don't be tempted to rush through these last few bits – give them as much time as you would any other stage to ensure you maintain a high standard throughout the process.

The method Neil used to paint the yellow is a particularly interesting technique as it is only three stages, but produces a very rich colour. It was also used on the other shoulder and knee pad of the model.

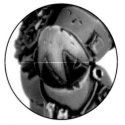

Yellow was used elsewhere on the model as a contrast to the grey armour.

The Shoulder Pad

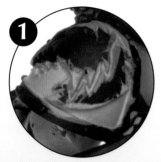

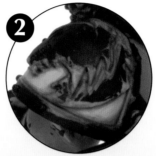

Step 1. Bubonic Brown was painted in the area of the shoulder pad between the rim and the raised Great Company symbol.

Step 2. This was highlighted with a 1:1 mix of Bubonic Brown and Bleached Bone, then washed with Ogryn Flesh and Gryphonne Sepia.

Step 3. A highlight of Bleached Bone, followed by a 1:1 mix of Bleached Bone and Skull White was applied. The icon was repainted black.

The Metal

Step 1. The metal rims of the shoulder pads were basecoated with a layer of Boltgun Metal.

Step 2. A wash of Devlan Mud was then applied to the rim. Be careful when applying the wash so run-off doesn't contaminate the yellow area.

Step 3. A Mithril Silver highlight was applied to the edges of the rim, onto the rivets, and as small scratches on the metal areas.

The Backpack

Step 1. The ornate wolf heads were first painted with a 3:1 basecoat mix of Shining Gold and Bestial Brown.

Step 2. The heads were highlighted with Shining Gold, followed by a wash of Ogryn Flesh.

Step 3. A highlight of Burnished Gold was applied, followed by a highlight with a 1:1 mix of Burnished Gold and Mithril Silver.

Painting the Belt

The Wolf Guard's belt really stands out due to the glowing runes. This effect is achieved by framing the glowing area, in this case a rune, with a darker shade of the main colour. Each subsequent layer should then be lighter in tone and shrink towards the source of the illumination.

The skull in the centre of the belt was first painted Bestial Brown followed by a layer of Snakebite Leather. The second stage was built up with a layer of Vomit Brown followed by Bleached Bone, then given a wash of Ogryn Flesh before receiving a final highlight of Skull White.

Belt and Runes

Step 1. The runes were first painted Regal Blue and then worked up with a 3:1 mix of Regal Blue and Ice Blue.

Step 2. Next, they were painted with a 1:1 mix of Regal Blue and Ice Blue; this was followed by layer of pure Ice Blue.

Step 3. The runes were highlighted with Space Wolves Grey and then a final, extreme highlight of Skull White.

Finishing Touches

Cabling
The cable stripes were painted Scab Red to create a red and black alternating pattern. A line of Codex Grey was painted along the whole area to simulate a reflection, which was highlighted with Fortress Grey.

Sculpted Base
The Ork icons on the base were painted in a similar manner to the metal rims of the shoulder pads, the only difference being that a Badab Black wash was used instead of Devlan Mud.

Chest Gem
The gems on the model were painted Red Gore, then Blood Red. This was followed by highlights of Blazing Orange and Vomit Brown. An extreme highlight of Bleached Bone and finally Skull White was then applied.

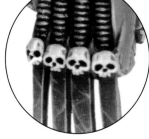

Skulls
These were painted using the same method as for the belt skull but a slightly heavier layer of Bleached Bone was used to give them a lighter tone.

THE COUNCIL OF ELROND™

'Eavy Metal stalwart Neil Green steps forth to answer the call in this Masterclass featuring that wisest of Elves, Elrond Half-Elven, including tips for painting freehand.

ELROND, MASTER OF RIVENDELL

Elrond Half-Elven is a pivotal figure in Tolkien mythology – an Elf Lord steeped in the blood of countless slain Orcs, who has survived some of the bleakest times to beset Middle-earth.

As the Third Age draws to a close and Sauron attempts to extend his domain, Elrond remains ready to rally the Free Peoples if, or more pertinently, when, the need should arise. In this age, Elrond has taken the role of mediator and counsellor. In his home of Rivendell, he welcomes all travellers of a good heart to set aside their burdens and rest their weary bones.

While he is a peaceful individual, Sauron should be wary. Elrond may have set aside his blade, but he is more than prepared to take it up once again should evil creatures threaten his home or allies.

A figure of incredible wisdom, Elrond features strongly in the decision to send the One Ring to Mount Doom in the hands of a humble Hobbit. It comes as no surprise to lovers of the book that the decision comes at the Council of Elrond.

Impressed by the character and the scenes in the movie where Elrond gathers the Fellowship and instructs them of their task, Gary Morley sculpted this Elrond miniature, Elrond Master of Rivendell. Whilst he is clad in the soft, elegant robes of an Elf at peace, one such as Elrond is never without means to defend himself.

For the honour of painting such an iconic character from The Lord of the RIngs we turned to Neil Green, veteran 'Eavy Metal painter and author of many Masterclass articles over the years.

No stranger to challenges such as these, Neil is happy to demonstrate his brush skills in this Masterclass, pointing out that the Elrond, Master of Rivendell miniature presented a great opportunity to demonstrate clean, smooth areas of cloth and intricate, detailed freehand patterns.

His first job was to meticulously clean the model up, carefully removing all the mould lines. He then stuck the model onto a base and sprayed it Chaos Black, using very short bursts to get maximum coverage.

The Fellowship of the Ring – Rivendell

Elrond is present throughout the story of *The Lord of the Rings*. His most notable appearance is, of course, at the Council of Elrond. As we've mentioned before, the great thing about *The Lord of the Rings* movies is that they provide a great visual reference for painting. The Elrond figure above has been painted in a palette of colours heavily inspired by the costume worn by Elrond (played by Hugo Weaving) in the Council scene.

The Return of the King – The Grey Havens

As we already had an Elrond in garb from *The Fellowship of the Ring*, for this Masterclass we decided to paint his robes as he was dressed at the Grey Havens in *The Return of the King*. The colours Neil uses form a palette of pale greys and neutral tones. These colours can be an effective scheme but will need an expert eye to achieve.

Painting flesh can be quite challenging and patience will be required to get the best look. If the paint goes on too thickly it will cake and you'll lose any pretence of a flesh tone. Neil paints flesh in lots of thin layers, applying two to three thin coats of watered-down paint rather than a single thick coat. This ensures the flesh is given a smooth, vibrant finish.

Shading and Highlights

This movie still is a great visual reference to see how light and shadow falls upon a face. The light source in this picture is coming from just above and slightly to the right, casting the right side of Elrond's face in shadow, particularly in the recessed areas around the eyes and close to the nose.

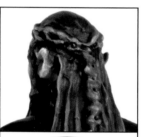

Hair

Neil started with a 1:1 basecoat mix of Scorched Brown and Chaos Black. He then applied a coat of pure Scorched Brown on all but the most recessed areas. The highlight was a 1:1 mix of Scorched Brown and Bleached Bone followed by the same mix, but adding even more Bleached Bone.

Painting the Face

Step 1. *Neil started with a basecoat using a 3:1 mix of Vermin Brown and Liche Purple.*

Step 2. *For the next stage he started with the same mix as before but added half as much again of Dwarf Flesh. This was painted on all the areas not in shadow.*

Step 3. *A mid-tone layer of pure Dwarf Flesh was then applied to the face. Again, the raised and prominent areas were covered but not the recessed areas.*

Step 4. *The first highlight layer was then brushed onto the prominent areas of the face. Neil used a 3:1 mix of Dwarf Flesh and Skull White for this stage.*

Step 5. *A further highlight was carefully blended onto the raised parts of the face using a 1:1 mix of Dwarf Flesh and Skull White.*

Step 6. *Finally, Neil painted the eyes. By dotting Bleached Bone into either side of the eye slit the pupil was formed.*

You should always plan out your colours before you set to painting, and this is especially true for clothing. As we discussed earlier, we're painting this version of Elrond as he appears at the end of *The Return of the King* movie. There is, of course, nothing stopping you from painting your version of Elrond in any colours you see fit.

The two references we have are in russet brown and neutral greys, but your imagination is the only limit and you could clothe him in rich green robes or cool blues, for example. Whichever colour scheme you choose, make sure you have a contrasting colour. A contrast is important as it helps the eye to define the model.

Painting the Blue Cloth

Step 1. To start with, Neil used a 2:1:1 mix of Regal Blue, Chaos Black and Ultramarines Blue as the basecoat.

Step 2. For the mid-tone, Neil added a little Bleached Bone to the mix in the following proportions: 3:1 blue mix to Bleached Bone.

Step 3. For the next layer, Neil repeated the previous stage but added more Bleached Bone, before carefully blending the layer as a highlight.

Step 4. For the edge highlight, Neil continued to use the same mix with even more Bleached Bone added: about 3:1 Bleached Bone to blue mix.

Painting the Metal

Step 1. The blade started with a 1:1 basecoat mix of Boltgun Metal and Chaos Black. A 1:1 mix of Shining Gold and Scorched Brown was used for the hilt.

Step 2. Neil then used washes for shading both parts of the sword – Badab Black for the blade and Devlan Mud for the hilt.

Step 3. A liberal layer of Chainmail was brushed onto the blade. The hilt was given a coat of Shining Gold.

Step 4. The hilt was highlighted with a 1:1 mix of Shining Gold and Mithril Silver, while the blade was highlighted with pure Mithril Silver.

Highlighting cloth requires a different technique to extreme edge highlighting. When you have a hard or flat surface like a sword blade or armour plates, then using an extreme highlight (a thin line using a lighter colour to the base for a distinctive contrast) is an effective technique. However, for softer, organic surfaces, such as cloth or foliage, then a subtler effect is called for.

So, for the robes, Neil achieved a three-dimensional effect by blending mid-tones, steadily progressing to the lighter colours until he was working purely with Skull White. Even then he used the Skull White very sparingly, only applying it to the seams and the very edge of the robe so it's almost indistinguishable to the previous layer – the opposite effect to an extreme highlight.

Thinning Paint

There can be nothing simpler than watering down paint, right? Well, when painting to the 'Eavy Metal standard, even this is a very clinical act to ensure consistency throughout the many stages and layers. Neil starts with a 1:1 mix of water and paint and from there will either thicken or water down depending on the task at hand. If covering a large area, such as the back of Elrond's robes, he'll water down the paint further. The larger the area, the thinner the paint.

Painting the Cloak

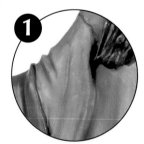

Step 1. A basecoat of Codex Grey was applied to the robes that had not already been painted blue.

Step 2. Neil then applied a shading wash of Devlan Mud directly into the recessed areas.

Step 3. A mid-tone using a 1:1 mix of Fortress Grey and Codex Grey was then applied to all but the most recessed areas.

Step 4. A lighter tone was blended to all but the most recessed areas, as in Step 3, using a thin coat of Fortress Grey.

Step 5. A third layer was added, using a 1:1 mix of Fortress Grey and Skull White. This was only used on the uppermost areas.

Step 6. A final highlight of Skull White was carefully applied to the most prominent folds of the robes.

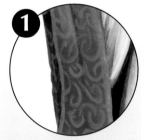

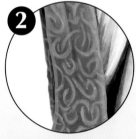

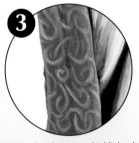

Practice Makes Perfect

Adding the final details, such as the patterning on Elrond's robe will take time and a steady hand. Neil, as an 'Eavy Metal painter, is obviously skilled at this kind of work – however, don't feel intimidated. You can leave the patterns off, go for a simpler design, or bite the bullet and try it. Get the pattern planned out before you begin – draw or paint it on a separate piece of paper. Remember, you can always paint over your mistakes!

Practising the designs on a piece of paper or card will save you from spoiling your efforts.

Painting the Sleeve Patterns

Step 1. Use the blue mix from earlier – (2:1:1 mix Regal Blue, Chaos Black & Ultramarines Blue).

Step 2. As before, Bleached Bone was added to the blue mix. (1:1 Bleached Bone to blue).

Step 3. The sleeve was highlighted with Bleached Bone, before being shaded with thinned Devlan Mud.

The finished Elrond model standing alongside his closest friends and allies.

URIEN RAKARTH

Juan Diaz's brilliantly sculpted Urien Rakarth miniature is the subject of this exclusive Dark Eldar Masterclass by Anja Wettergren.

The Haemonculi of Commorragh are dark-hearted torturers. They are connoisseurs of pain who spend centuries crafting symphonies of agony within their secret lairs deep in the bowels of the Dark City. The covens of the Haemonculi are integral to Commorrite society due to their mastery of regenerative practices, yet they remain figures of terror and suspicion. The appearance of a Haemonculus no doubt adds to the air of terror for they have experimented on themselves as much as their 'clients' and have taken on a terrifying aspect. Spines jut from their backs and move independently, internal organs are kept in fleshy sacks and their sparse alabaster frames have not an ounce of fat upon them.

Of all the Haemonculi none is more feared than the father of pain himself, Urien Rakarth. Floating majestically across the battlefield, carried by flesh hungry haemovores that constantly writhe about beneath him, Rakarth scours realspace ever keen to gather fresh subjects and release his latest creations upon the poor innocents of the galaxy.

'Eavy Metal's Anja Wettergren elected to paint the grand torturer for this Masterclass. In fitting with the look of the model she has selected pallid and purple tones, with complementary greens and blues. Within the Dark Eldar army Urien will stand out as his pale tones will contrast well against the dark armour of the Kabalite Warriors.

The colours also suit the aesthetics of the figure. Juan has sculpted a very finely detailed model; this is no Space Marine and so bright primary colours would be too drastic, a metaphorical punch in the gut instead of a light slap on the wrist. The tonal palette Anja has chosen works well because it enhances the delicate style of the model.

As well as the elegant paintwork, the miniature also offered Anja the chance to showcase an oft-requested technique: how to paint glass. Rakarth is bedecked in phials, syringes and drips hang menacingly from his atrophied appendages, all contain some potent mutagenic liquids. These offer plenty of opportunities to try out a technique for painting liquids in glass.

Starting the Model

After cleaning up the figure by removing the flash and placing the model on a slottabase, Anja gave it a Chaos Black undercoat. When the undercoat was dry, the miniature was ready for painting in earnest. To ensure a consistent look Anja works in a very methodical way, painting all the areas that share the same method before moving on to another part of the model. For instance, she basecoated all the skin areas at the same time, then applied the shading stage, and so on. Only when all the flesh was complete did Anja move on to the next area.

As a rule, you should paint from the inside outwards, starting with areas such as the flesh and moving up through cloth and armour. Painting in this order will prevent you from accidentally covering areas that have already been painted, and it means that as you work outwards you'll be able to paint over areas that may have caught the odd brush stroke.

Painting the Flesh

Step 1. *Anja started by basecoating all the flesh areas with a 1:1 mix of Tallarn Flesh and Space Wolves Grey.*

Step 2. *She then created a Dark Flesh glaze and applied that into the recesses, followed by a wash of Devlan Mud.*

Step 3. *A mid-tone using the mix from Stage 1 with equal parts Skull White was then painted onto the flesh.*

Step 4. *More Skull White was added to the previous mix, which Anja then applied over several thin highlight layers.*

Step 5. *Anja then created a Leviathan Purple glaze and applied this directly into the recesses of the skin.*

Step 6. *Finally, a fine highlight of pure Skull White was applied to the most prominent parts of the flesh.*

Painting the Coat Lining

Step 1. *Anja first painted the area using a 4:3:3 mix of Scab Red, Chaos Black and Liche Purple.*

Step 2. *Next, she added a line highlight of Scab Red towards the trim of the cloak.*

Step 3. *She then applied a thin highlight of Blood Red, again on the trim of the cloak.*

Step 4. *Finally, a highlight of Dwarf Flesh was carefully applied to the very edge of the cloak.*

Painting the Attire

While Rakarth will have his own agenda when partaking in a realspace raid, he remains a part of the Dark Eldar army and so the armour on the miniature is a good way of tying him to the rest of the force. With this in mind, Anja painted the armour to match in a similar style to the rest of the Studio collection. This means painting the armour plates in very dark, almost-black tones with bright flashes of colour on the trim, giving the armour a 'neon' look that is both aesthetically pleasing and yet still sinister. It also works well with the colour palette on the rest of the model adding a stark contrast to the pallid flesh tones and the apron when they're painted later in the process.

One of Rakarth's many arms is covered in a gauntlet and Anja has used the same method to paint this as the segmented armour on the torso. Wherever the armour is ridged or forms a peak, most notably on the knuckles of the gauntlet and the abdominal area of the torso, the contrast is the starkest, thus giving the desired effect.

Painting the Armour

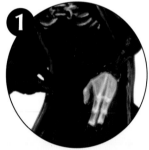

Step 1. *Anja started by basecoating the armour using a 1:1:2 mix of Dark Angels Green, Enchanted Blue and Chaos Black.*

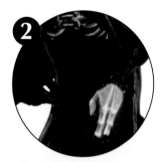

Step 2. *Chaos Black was then thinned down with a small amount of water and applied directly into the recesses of the armour.*

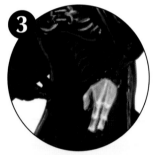

Step 3. *Using a 1:1 mix of Dark Angels Green and Enchanted Blue, Anja applied the paint to the edge of every armour segment.*

Step 4. *A finer highlight was then applied, using a 6:2:1:1 of Rotting Flesh, Scorpion Green, Enchanted Blue and Dark Angels Green.*

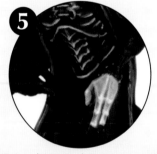

Step 5. *Anja then painted on pure Rotting Flesh as an even finer highlight working her way to the very edges of the armour plates.*

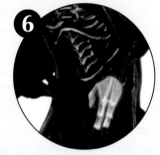

Step 6. *Finally, on only the most prominent edges, Anja painted a fine highlight with a 1:1 mix of Rotting Flesh and Skull White.*

Painting the Outside of the Coat

Step 1. *The coat's exterior was first painted with a 1:1 mix of Chaos Black and Rotting Flesh.*

Step 2. *More Rotting Flesh was added to the previous mix and then was layered onto the coat.*

Step 3. *Rotting Flesh was added again to the same mix, applied to the raised folds of the coat.*

Step 4. *A fresh mix using equal parts Skull White and Rotting Flesh was used as a final highlight.*

Painting the Glass Phials

The trick to painting phials is to remember that the liquid inside is always parallel to the horizon. So even if the container is at an angle, the liquid should still be painted level with the base. Highlights are then applied towards the top level of the liquid, in a very similar fashion to painting gems. To give the impression of glass, carefully paint thin lines Skull White around the end of the cylinder and along it.

Step 1. The blue liquid was painted Regal Blue; the green fluid was painted with Dark Angels Green.

Step 2. Anja then started to layer the blue fluid with Enchanted Blue and the green liquid with Snot Green.

Step 3. A 1:1 mix of Enchanted Blue and Ice Blue was then applied to the blue; Scorpion Green layered on the green.

Step 4. Pure Ice Blue was layered onto the blue liquid, a 1:1 mix of Sunburst Yellow and Scorpion Green was also used.

Step 5. Space Wolves Grey was layered on the blue liquid; the green used the previous mix with Skull White added.

Step 6. Skull White was applied on both phials as described above to create a glass effect.

The red fluid used a Scab Red base and was then highlighted using Red Gore, Blood Red and then to Blazing Orange.

The fluid in the syringe was painted using the same method as for the green liquid – note the angle of the liquid.

'EAVY METAL™ GLASS EFFECTS SHOWCASE

You'll find glass or material that looks like glass on many models. Whether it's a searchlight, targeter lens or an hourglass, knowing how to paint glass is always a useful technique to have in your repertoire. Here are a few more examples.

This Ratling is busy spying out his next target. A coat of gloss varnish helps pick out the lens.

The poisoned wind globes on this Skaven have been painted as though filled with swirling clouds of gas.

The searchlight and phial on this Apothecary have all been painted to suggest a glass effect.

The Amethyst Wizard's hourglass has had thin coats of gloss varnish applied to make it shine.

Painting the Extremities

One of the many unsettling abnormalities on the miniature are the tentacle-like haemovores that swarm around Rakarth's feet and seem to carry the Master Haemonculus forward. Anja has painted these in rich reds rather than in the same flesh tones of Rakarth as this gives a good counterpoint to the skin and yet compliments the overall paint scheme, echoing the reds found on the trim of the coat and fluid in the tubes.

The haemovores' ridged and segmented forms lend themselves perfectly to shading and highlighting. This has allowed Anja to subtly inject a slight purple tone into the shading of the red, which helps tie the whole model together.

The weapon carried by the Master Haemonculus is an exaggerated surgical blade so Anja has painted it as such, keeping it very clean and shiny, with very little shading. Equally you could imagine the blade to be corroded or blood splattered but that's a decision each painter will have to make.

Painting the Haemovores

Step 1. Anja started by basecoating the haemovores with a 1:1:1 mix of Red Gore, Liche Purple and Chaos Black.

Step 2. She then layered on pure Red Gore, applying it to the ridges, avoiding the recesses.

Step 3. Anja then started to build up the highlights, first starting with a 1:1 mix of Red Gore and Kommando Khaki.

Step 4. Yet more Kommando Khaki was added to the mix and this was then applied over the previous highlight.

Step 5. Anja then made a red glaze by mixing Baal Red with water and applying this over all the haemovores.

Step 6. The mix from Step 4 was then reapplied. She then added Skull White to the mix and used this as the final highlight.

Painting the Metals

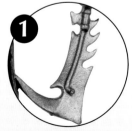 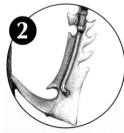 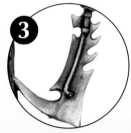 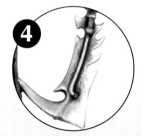

Step 1. Anja basecoated the wicked-looking blade with Boltgun Metal.

Step 2. Chainmail was then layered on to the blade.

Step 3. A wash of Liche Purple, Red Gore and Chaos Black was applied, followed by Ogryn Flesh.

Step 4. To finish, the weapon was highlighted with Mithril Silver around the edges.

The mass of flesh, arms and spines protruding behind Rakarth's head was all painted in the same flesh tones as the head and feet.

The claw was painted in the same way as the blade, but with more of the wash shade applied to, and around, the metal joints.

The apron is made from scraps of stitched-together flayed skin. To get the patchwork look, Anja used different basecoats for each piece of skin and then treated it as one area for the following shading and highlight stages. For the basecoats she used pure Tallarn Flesh, a 1:1 mix of Tallarn Flesh and Dark Flesh, and a 1:1 mix of Tallarn Flesh and Snakebite Leather.

The completed Urien Rakarth in all his vile glory. Note how the green in the syringe, around the head and on the tubes makes for a good spot colour.

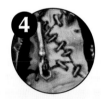

The face is gruesomely stretched over the skull. The exposed skull was painted up from Dheneb Stone blending in Bleached Bone.

Painting Flayed Skin

Step 1. Anja basecoated each segment of skin in one of three tones, as described above.

Step 2. A shade using a 1:1 mix of Liche Purple and Scorched Brown was painted into the recesses.

Step 3. Rotting Flesh was added to the basecoat and this was then used to highlight the matching segment of skin.

Step 4. Pure Rotting Flesh was then used by Anja to highlight the whole apron and paint the stitches.

Step 5. She then made a 1:1 mix of Rotting Flesh and Skull White and continued to highlight the apron.

Step 6. Finally, Anja used pure Skull White highlighting around the edges and stitching of the apron.

Painting Hair

Step 1. Anja basecoated the hair with a 1:1 mix of Chaos Black and Ice Blue.

Step 2. Ice Blue was added to the previous mix and this was painted directly onto the strands of hair.

Step 3. More Ice Blue was then added to the mix and this was painted on as a finer highlight.

Step 4. A 1:1 mix of Ice Blue and Space Wolves Grey was applied to the most prominent strands.

SKAVEN

VERMIN LORD

WARHAMMER®

Joe Tomaszewski offered to paint us a Skaven Vermin Lord for this Masterclass. In addition to reminding us of this fantastic classic miniature, he also gaves us an in-depth tutorial on directional lighting.

There are few sights to terrify the enemies of the Skaven like a Vermin Lord, a Daemon incarnate of the Horned Rat. These horrific creatures exude an aura of malicious might and inscrutable knowledge. They are at once majestic and disgusting, a living icon of ruin and the ultimate scavenger.

Michael Perry's classic sculpt of the Vermin Lord is well over 15 years old, yet it retains a menacing appearance and characteristic silhouette that fits perfectly with the recent Skaven models designed by the likes of Brian Nelson, Seb Perbet and Colin Grayson.

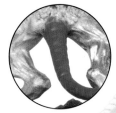

We set the challenge of painting up this classic miniature to 'Eavy Metal's Joe Tomaszewski, a task he took to with relish. He began by assembling the model, pinning the metal components in place. Joe decided to make two conversions to this model, which you can see to the right. Firstly, he replaced the head of the glaive with one he's made out of plasticard, because he wanted the weapon blade to match the weapons from the new plastic Stormvermin more closely. Secondly, because he chose to put the model on a large (50mm) base, with rocks for extra height, he felt that the model was a bit unbalanced, so he extended the tail with Green Stuff. As you can see, Joe's quite the perfectionist!

Painting the Flesh and Fur

Joe gave the Vermin Lord a bit of extra height with the addition of some plasticard rocks, adding to the Vermin Lord's already impressive stature. To make the model even more imposing, Joe used a large monster base instead of the usual 40mm square one, and the rocks really helped to break up this larger base area. A couple of plastic rats gleaned from various kits grounded the model in a mini-narrative.

Once the base was finished, the model was undercoated with Chaos Black Spray. Joe started work by painting the flesh and fur. To get a definite contrast between the two areas, the flesh was painted in pale browns and the fur in a black tone with grey highlights. It's always best practice to paint models from the 'inside out,' so that there's less chance of making mistakes or splashing colours on areas that have already been painted. For this reason, Joe painted the flesh first before moving on to the fur. He painted the skin using the common method of applying a solid basecoat, followed by a wash to shade it, and then blending the highlights with continually lighter colours.

The Skin

Step 1. Joe started by applying a solid basecoat, using a 1:1 mix of Tallarn Flesh and Calthan Brown.

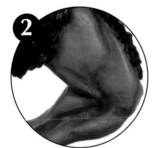

Step 2. A 1:1 mix of Scorched Brown and Chaos Black was thinned down and applied as a wash over the whole area, especially in the recesses.

Step 3. The basecoat mix was reapplied to all but the recessed areas. When dry this was followed by an application of pure Tallarn Flesh.

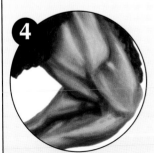

Step 4. A 1:1 mix of Tallarn Flesh and Bleached Bone was layered onto the area. Pure Bleached Bone was then applied in the same fashion.

Step 5. The final blend consisted of a 1:1 mix of Skull White and Bleached Bone, applied to the more prominent areas of the flesh.

Step 6. To add life and lustre to the skin, Scab Red and Liche Purple glazes were applied into some of the recesses, and mottled onto part of the skin.

The Fur

Step 1. A 1:1 mix of Codex Grey and Chaos Black was overbrushed onto the fur.

Step 2. Pure Codex Grey was carefully painted onto the raised clumps of hair.

Step 3. A final highlight using a 3:1 mix of Fortress Grey and Skull White was then applied.

Painting the Skull, Horns and Hooves

There are two common methods of blending highlights that the 'Eavy Metal team use time and time again. The first is to start with a dark basecoat and then blend the highlights progressively, before finishing off with a fine edge highlight. You can see this method used expertly on the Vermin Lord's hooves (on the next page). The other method has become more popular since the Foundation paints were released. Rather than starting with a dark colour and painting up to lighter tones, they sometimes start with a light Foundation colour, such as Dheneb Stone. They then apply a shading wash before blending back to the mid-tone. This saves on numerous stages of blending and 'maps out' the shades from the wash stage onwards, making the mid-tone steps easier to apply. Joe has used this method on the horns and the skull.

The traditional dark-to-light blending method results in a darker overall finish, often with strong contrasts and a stark highlight. The basecoat and wash method leaves you with a lighter overall finish, which is perfect for large, smooth areas, or for any part of a miniature that you need to stand out with lighter tones such as, for example, the Vermin Lord's large skull face.

The Skull

Step 1. *The exposed half of the skull was first painted with a 1:1 mix of Astronomican Grey and Dheneb Stone.*

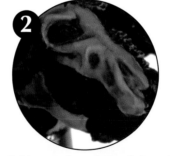

Step 2. *A heavy wash was then applied over the basecoat using a 3:1 mix of Devlan Mud and Asurmen Blue.*

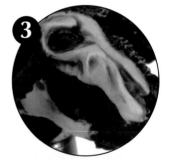

Step 3. *The original 1:1 mix of Astronomican Grey and Dheneb Stone was reapplied to all but the most recessed areas of the skull.*

Step 4. *The skull was then highlighted, first with a 1:1:2 mix of Astronomican Grey, Dheneb Stone and Skull White.*

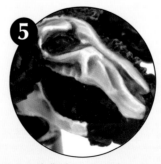

Step 5. *Pure Skull White was used as a fine highlight, applied to the most prominent areas of the exposed skull.*

Step 6. *Chips and cracks in the bone were carefully painted onto the skull using a 1:1 mix of Scorched Brown and Chaos Black, and accentuated with Skull White.*

The Horns

 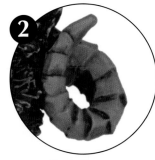 

Step 1. The horns of the Vermin Lord were given a basecoat of Astronomican Grey.

Step 2. A liberal wash of Badab Black was brushed all over the horns, concentrating on the recesses beneath the ridges.

Step 3. A coat of Astronomican Grey was then reapplied, covering all but the recessed areas under the ridges.

Step 4. A Chaos Black glaze was brushed all over the horn. The glaze layer was then built up over subsequent coats, working towards the tip of the horn until that was a solid black.

Step 5. A hard edge highlight using a 1:1 mix of Astronomican Grey and Skull White was then applied to the prominent points of the horn.

Step 6. A few chips and cracks were carefully applied using a 1:1 mix of Scorched Brown and Chaos Black, before being underscored with Skull White.

The Hooves (and Claws)

Step 1. The hooves were basecoated with a 1:1:1 mix of Scorched Brown, Chaos Black and Dheneb Stone.

Step 2. Codex Grey was incrementally added to the previous mix and blended towards the outside of the hooves.

Step 3. Thin vertical lines were painted onto the hooves using a 1:1 mix of Codex Grey and Fortress Grey.

Step 4. The lines and the edges of the hooves were then highlighted with pure Fortress Grey.

Step 5. A 1:1 mix of Fortress Grey and Skull White was used to repeat the previous step, highlighting the vertical lines and edges.

Step 6. A 1:1 mix of Scorched Brown and Chaos Black was used to create a few grooves and chips in the hooves. These effects were accentuated with Skull White.

Painting Metal

The Vermin Lord is the very embodiment of the foul, pestilent race that is the Skaven, and Joe has used many of the techniques on this model that he developed while working on the Studio Skaven army. The metallic areas are a great case in point – most Skaven weapons are old, scavenged and corroded, and Joe paints them in a dull, dark metal colour, complete with oxidation and blemishes. Even the Vermin Lord's adornments look older and more worn than the decoration favoured by other races.

As is often the case, real world reference is always ideal for research purposes. Old bits of iron, or just reference pictures can really help when applying rust or weathering effects, as you can see how dull the metal becomes, and where spots of rust and verdigris form.

Careful use of washes can dull down metallic paints to give them an old and worn look, be careful of over-using this technique or else you will matt down the metal areas too much, and they will look more grey than silver, or yellow/brown rather than gold.

The Collar

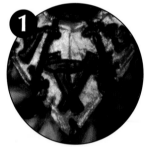

Step 1. A basecoat of Dwarf Bronze was applied onto the collar in a solid coat.

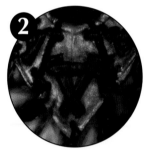

Step 2. A Devlan Mud wash was then brushed over the whole area with extra shading applied close to raised details.

Step 3. A 1:1 mix of Chainmail and Dwarf Bronze was used as an initial highlight, painted onto the edges and around the scratches and nicks.

Step 4. Pure Chainmail was used as the final highlight as well as to paint chips onto the surface of the collar.

Step 5. To add depth to the area, a Liche Purple glaze was applied in random patches around the collar.

Step 6. A 3:1 glaze of Hawk Turquoise and Chaos Black was painted on in a similar style to the purple glaze.

The Bells

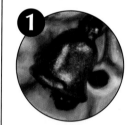

Step 1. The bell was first painted with Tin Bitz.

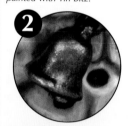

Step 2. The bell was then highlighted with a 1:1 mix of Tin Bitz and Chainmail.

Step 3. Finally, the bell was given a Devlan Mud wash and a Chainmail highlight.

Painting the Doomglaive

The Blade

The original blade of the doomglaive was replaced with this one, carefully fashioned from plasticard.

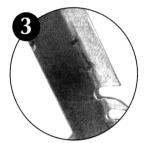

Step 1. A basecoat using a 1:1 mix of Boltgun Metal and Chaos Black was painted on the blade.

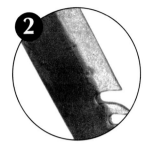

Step 2. This was blended up to pure Boltgun Metal over several thin coats.

Step 3. Chainmail was blended onto the blade, and also applied as a hard highlight along the edge.

Step 4. The blade was dulled down with a mixture of Liche Purple and Chaos Black glazes.

Step 5. To create an oxidisation effect, a 3:1 mixture of Hawk Turquoise and Chaos Black was stippled onto parts of the blade.

Step 6. Skull White was added to the previous mix and then applied in spots and mottled areas on certain parts of the blade.

The Haft

Step 1. The haft was basecoated with a 1:1 mix of Scorched Brown and Chaos Black.

Step 2. Pure Scorched Brown was applied along the wood grain, avoiding the troughs and recessed channels.

Step 3. A 1:1 mix of Scorched Brown and Vomit Brown was applied as a highlight to the raised areas of the haft.

Step 4. Finally, a 1:1 mix of Vomit Brown and Bleached Bone was used on the most prominent parts of the grain.

The Strapping

Step 1. The strapping on the handle was first basecoated with Bleached Bone.

Step 2. A Devlan Mud wash was then brushed over the area.

Step 3. Bleached Bone was reapplied to all but the recessed parts of the strapping.

Step 4. A 1:1 mix of Bleached Bone and Skull White was used as the final highlight.

DIRECTIONAL LIGHTING

Directional lighting, also known as Object Source Lighting (or OSL in miniature painting circles), is an advanced technique that involves creating the illusion of an additional light source on a miniature in addition to the natural light. The source of the effect can vary depending on the model. Naked flames, torches, LEDs, power weapons and magical items might all generate light.

What's the Theory?

Directional lighting is best applied after the model has been finished in all other respects, as the light will affect the colours it's painted onto. The source of the lighting (a flame or lamp, for example) should be the brightest part of the model with the hue it projects gradually fading the further away it radiates from the originating point.

How's it Done?

Because of their translucent nature, glazes are a good medium for painting reflected hues on top of existing colours. This is the method Joe used on the Vermin Lord, because it's a light colour shining onto pale surfaces.

Another option is to mix the primary colour of the light source into the paint mix used on the area the light is hitting. As the colour fades out the further it is from the source you add more of the original mix in. This is the best option when dealing with darker surfaces where glazes will not show up clearly. This can be a tricky procedure as the area you are applying the effect onto will already have been shaded and highlighted. Unfortunately, there are no hidden short cuts – you simply have to take the differing shades and highlights into consideration and adjust your light sourcing mix accordingly. For example, if you were to paint a red light effect onto green cloth you need to mix the red with the green mid-tone, the highlight mix and the shade mix, applying it wherever the light would naturally spill across all three areas of the material.

It will take time and more than a little patience to apply this, depending on both the size of the light source and affected area, but when this is done you can work to making the effect more prominent. This is achieved by highlighting back towards the source, building on the hues you have already blended in. For instance, with a flame, you could go from a dark red to a mid-tone red, then orange, to yellow and finally white on the area right next to the light source. When dealing with the brightest hues, be careful not to make the effect brighter or more glaring than the actual light source as that can ruin the illusion.

Painting directional lighting onto dark colours will always look more convincing so you should consider this when planning what colour to paint your miniature with. For example, if you wish to have light from a burning brand spilling onto a shield, then you should think about painting the shield in a dark colour such as dark green or blue. That's not to say applying directional lighting onto light areas is inferior, but there is no denying that it is more difficult to pull off.

When painting this effect you need to always keep in mind the shape of the model and how the light will fall on these surfaces. Don't assume that light radiates out in an even circle from the source because it rarely reacts in such a neat manner. A good tip is to shine a small amount of light onto the model from a torch and take note of where light bounces off and which parts remain covered in shadow. A little practice will give you a convincing effect.

The sigils on the Vermin Lord's collar all glow with the menacing light of warpstone. Joe has used the method described on the next page to achieve this effect.

For the Wizard Painting Challenge in July 2009's White Dwarf, Fil Dunn used a very effective directional lighting technique on his Light Wizard. He actually shined a small torch directly down onto the miniature to see where the light would spill.

Light Hues

Here are a few suggestions of the highlight tones you could work through to get a convincing OSL effect. Start with the dark colours and work inwards, getting lighter towards the light source.

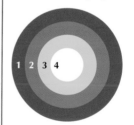

Red (flame)
1. Blood Red
2. Blazing Orange
3. Sunburst Yellow
4. Skull White

Green (eerie glow)
1. Dark Angels Green
2. Snot Green
3. Sunburst Yellow
4. Skull White

Yellow (searchlight)
1. Golden Yellow
2. Sunburst Yellow
3. Skull White

Blue (power weapon)
1. Regal Blue
2. Enchanted Blue
3. Ice Blue
4. Skull White

You can see some brilliant examples of Object Source Lighting on page 59.

Painting the Warpstone

Joe used a directional lighting effect on the warpstone chunks embedded into the Vermin Lord. Joe was aiming for a more subtle, malignant glow than a bright flare of light caused by a flame or lantern and so used a series of glazes to prime the lighted areas rather than blending the light source with an existing mix. The light radius is kept deliberately small although the effect still looks striking due to the multiple shards and Joe's skill with the brush. As he is working from a green light source he used dark green on the areas furthest away, working through to a mid-tone up to yellow and white on the areas closest to the warpstone.

The Warpstone

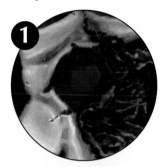
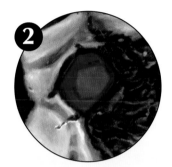
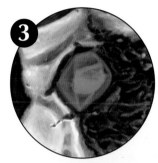

Step 1. The warpstone was basecoated with Orkhide Shade.

Step 2. Snot Green was then painted onto the warpstone over all but the most recessed areas, and underneath the corners and sharp edges.

Step 3. A 1:1 mix of Snot Green and Scorpion Green was applied to the raised areas and prominent edges of the shard.

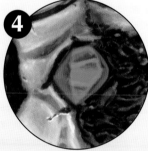
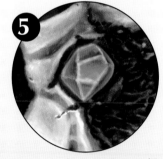
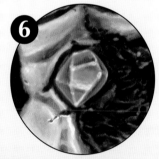

Step 4. Pure Scorpion Green was carefully used along the many edges of the warpstone.

Step 5. A 1:1 mix of Scorpion Green and Sunburst Yellow was then applied to the same edges.

Step 6. Joe picked out the sharpest points of the warpstone with pure Skull White.

Warpstone Glow

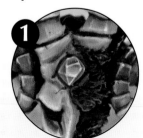

Step 1. Several glazes of Snot Green were applied in a half centimetre radius from the warpstone shard, getting stronger towards the centre.

Step 2. Highlights were applied to the glazed area with the careful application of Scorpion Green.

Step 3. Sunburst Yellow highlights followed, which were applied more strongly closer to the shard.

Step 4. Finally, the raised areas nearest the shard were highlighted with a fine edge of Skull White.

Painting the Tail

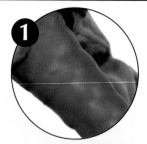

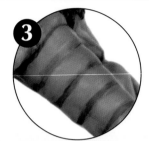

Step 1. A basecoat using a 1:1 mix of Tallarn Flesh and Scab Red was painted onto the tail.

Step 2. Devlan Mud was brushed over the area, concentrating on the dips between the ridges.

Step 3. A 3:1 mix of Tallarn Flesh and Scab Red was painted onto the tail leaving the channels uncovered.

Step 4. Lastly, a 1:1 mix of Tallarn Flesh and Bleached Bone was used to highlight the edges of the ridges.

Final Details

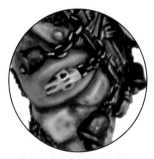

The small skulls dangling from the creature's chest were painted just like the exposed part of the Vermin Lord's skull. Joe used the metal effect as on the glaive for the chains.

Once painted, you can't even tell that the tail was scratch-built by Joe.

The eye was painted first Scab Red, then highlighted Blood Red, Sunburst Yellow and finally Skull White.

The fur on the Giant Rat had a basecoat of Scorched Brown, followed by a Devlan Mud wash. A highlight using a 1:1 mix of Scorched Brown and Bleached Bone was then applied. Its flesh was painted in the same way as the Vermin Lord's.

DIRECTONAL LIGHTING SHOWCASE

This Dark Elf Assassin, painted by Darren Latham, has a glowing phial hanging from his belt.

Another fine example of the technique is this dishevelled-looking Frodo by Luis Gomez Pradal.

The sigils on the side of this Bloodcrusher appear to be glowing, as though filled with molten metal.

The toxic gases within this Poisoned Wind Globadier's globe appear to be glowing balefully.

David Rodriguez is a master of the technique, as this gold-winning Golden Demon entry proves.

This 2001 Diorama by Victoria Lamb is a real masterclass in how lighting plays off different surfaces.

DAEMON PRINCE

Here Kornel Kozak goes toe-to-toe with the sorcerous might of a Daemon Prince, demonstrating how to paint colour fades in astonishing detail.

For those mortals who pledge their allegiance to the Dark Gods and devote their lives to the glory of Chaos, there is one reward that all desire above any other: to be blessed with the gift of immortality, to be raised to daemonhood and granted eternal life spent fighting for the delight of their patrons.

To gain the attentions of the Chaos Gods is no trivial feat, for a warrior must risk all for even the merest flicker of interest from their patrons. Armies must be ground into bloody ruin, thousands if not millions must be sacrificed and even then ascension is no sure thing. For the capricious Chaos Gods bestow mutations as a sign of their favour, and most find themselves overpowered by the bounty of such a blessing, their flesh sundered by the raw stuff of Chaos, changed forever into a heaving Chaos Spawn festooned with needle-studded tentacles, bulging eyeballs, drooling maws and chitinous claws.

Only the strongest of both mind and body can receive the gifts of Chaos and withstand the horrific flesh-change that it wreaks upon them. These champions of Chaos might one day attain daemonhood and grasp their place amongst the daemonic legions. Some will choose to remain amongst the realm of mortals, adored as physical representations of the power of Chaos, while others will fully

embrace their place within the Realm of Chaos, dwelling amongst the constantly warring Daemons as a new player in the Great Game of the Dark Gods.

The challenge of painting a Daemon Prince miniature is ripe with opportunity, for with the powers of Chaos anything is possible. That sense of adventure and unlimited potential really appeals to 'Eavy Metal's Kornel Kozak – he's got a keen love of the bright, vibrant colours featured amongst many of our armies, and relished the chance to try out a different palette on the Daemon Prince miniature.

For Kornel it wasn't enough just to paint the new model and show us how he went about it. He also wanted to demonstrate a painting technique that would be useful for painters of any stripe – how to achieve great-looking colour fades on models.

The technique of colour fading is where a painter painstakingly blends one colour into another creating a smooth transition to the new hue. This is a great way of showing the kaleidoscopic nature of the Daemons of Chaos or the shimmering eldritch tones of a Spirit Host or the Army of the Dead.

So, join me as we look at how Kornel unleashed his painting talents upon the Daemon Prince, creating a model with rich, vibrant colours that fade beautifully into one another.

Daemonic Flesh

Since most of the Daemon Prince miniature is flesh, Kornel tackled those areas of the model first, creating a strong starting point for the rest of the model. Over eight stages he painted, shaded and highlighted the Daemon's skin. Bear in mind that it's always better to do two thin coats than one thick coat when painting.

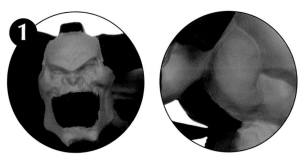

Step 1. The Daemon Prince's flesh was basecoated with a 2:1 mix of Dheneb Stone and Ice Blue.

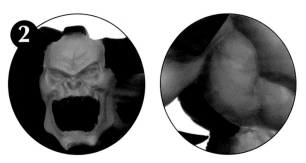

Step 2. Next Kornel added a little Regal Blue to the previous mix and, having watered it down, painted it carefully into the recesses as a shade to define the muscles and other raised details.

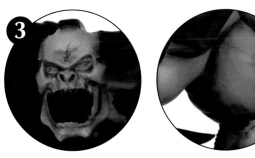

Step 3. A further shade, this time with a 2:2:1 mix of Scorched Brown, Liche Purple and Chaos Black was applied.

Step 4. Next, Kornel neated up the flesh with the original 2:1 mix of Dheneb Stone and Ice Blue.

Step 5. The raised areas of the Daemon Prince's skin were highlighted with a 3:1:1 mix of Dheneb Stone, Ice Blue and Kommando Khaki.

Step 6. The flesh was given a further highlight of Dheneb Stone and Skull White mixed 3:2.

Step 7. Another highlight, this time with a 1:1 mix of Dheneb Stone and Skull White, was then painted onto the Daemon Prince's flesh.

Step 8. A final highlight of pure Skull White was painted onto the face, after which the recesses around the eyes were washed with a 1:1:1 mix of Dark Angels Green, Goblin Green and Skull White. The flesh around the Daemon Prince's mouth was then washed with Baal Red and Scab Red mixed 1:1.

With the skin of the Daemon Prince painted, Kornel set about adding in the details to the model, including painting the armour plates and a colour fade on the clawed hands and feet of the Daemon Prince.

When painting a colour fade such as Kornel has done here, the trick is to always leave some of the colour from the previous stage showing to create a gradual transition. If you look carefully at the example on the leg shown below, you can see that as the stages progress towards the foot, the fade gets gradually darker the further down it goes.

You can achieve this effect by carefully watering down your paints and applying them as glazes – ideally you're looking for about the same consistency as a Citadel Wash. This glaze is then painted onto an area specifically to stain or colour it. You can see this very clearly on the Daemon Prince's legs.

While Citadel Washes are designed for shading models, you can also apply them as glazes by watering them down. Mixing them with a little paint can add to the vibrancy of the glaze. Remember: several thin layers are always better than one thick layer and will give the right 'fade' effect that we're looking for.

The Legs

Step 1. Kornel used three successive glazes of Kommando Khaki and Regal Blue mixed 2:1 on the lower legs.

Step 2. A little more Regal Blue was added into the previous mix. Kornel then glazed this onto the legs in two further coats.

Step 3. Kornel then added more Liche Purple into the previous glaze for an additional layer.

Step 4. A further glaze, was applied, adding a little more Liche Purple into the previous mix.

Step 5. Another glaze was made, this time with a small amount of Chaos Black added into the previous mix.

Step 6. A final glaze of pure Chaos Black was painted over the very bottom of the feet.

Step 7. The recesses were shaded with watered-down Chaos Black. The raised areas were highlighted using mixes from the flesh stage.

Step 8. A small amount of Space Wolves Grey was added to the previous mix for a fine highlight on the raised areas.

Armour Plates

Step 1. *Kornel basecoated the shoulder pad with a 1:1 mix of Regal Blue and Chaos Black.*

Step 2. *A highlight of Regal Blue was then painted around the etched details.*

Step 3. *Kornel then washed the highlight with watered-down Chaos Black.*

Step 4. *The inside edges of the highlight were highlighted, with a 2:2:1 mix of Regal Blue, Warlock Purple and Space Wolves Grey.*

Step 5. *The inside edge was given a further highlight using the previous mix with a little more Space Wolves Grey added in.*

Step 6. *Kornel used a final highlight of pure Space Wolves Grey was added to complete the detail.*

Golden Armour Trim

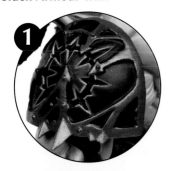

Step 1. *The armour trim was basecoated with a 1:1 mix of Scorched Brown and Shining Gold.*

Step 2. *The golden trim was then layered with Shining Gold.*

Step 3. *The recesses on the trim were washed using a 1:1 mix of Leviathan Purple and Ogryn Flesh.*

Step 4. *A further shade, this time of Devlan Mud was washed into the recesses.*

Step 5. *The edges were highlighted with a 1:1 mix of Burnished Gold and Shining Gold.*

Step 6. *Kornel then made a final highlight of pure Mithril Silver.*

The Daemonic Glow

Step 1. *The recesses and edges of the armour plates were painted with a basecoat of Dark Angels Green.*

Step 2. *A 1:1 mix of Dark Angels Green and Hawk Turquoise was used as a highlight, applied to the edges and inner recesses.*

Step 3. *Kornel added using the previous mix with a little Ice Blue added in.*

Step 4. *More Ice Blue, along with a little Skull White was added into the previous mix for the next highlight stage.*

Step 5. *A further touch of Skull White was added to the mix for the next highlight – the brightest areas towards the centre.*

Step 6. *Kornel painted a very fine highlight of pure Skull White to finish the glow. He then tidied up the armour by repainting parts of it, using the same colours as before.*

The Daemonic Blade

Step 1. *The sword was basecoated with a 1:1 mix of Liche Purple and Chaos Black.*

Step 2. *The outer edges of the blade were washed with watered-down Chaos Black.*

Step 3. *Liche Purple highlights were painted on, and several washes of watered-down Liche Purple were applied around them.*

Step 4. *The recessed details were painted with a 1:1 mix of Liche Purple and Ice Blue.*

Step 5. *The inner details were highlighted by adding a little Skull White into the previous mix.*

Step 6. *Even more Skull White was added to the previous mix and painted on as a final highlight. The whole blade was then glazed with a wash of Liche Purple.*

The Loincloth

Step 1. *The loincloth was basecoated with a 2:1 mix of Astronomican Grey and Shadow Grey.*

Step 2. *The whole loincloth was then washed with a watered-down Shadow Grey and Chaos Black, mixed 1:1.*

Step 3. *The recesses were shaded with an additional wash of the mix, with a little more Chaos Black added in.*

Step 4. *The raised areas were highlighted with a 1:1 mix of Astronomican Grey and Shadow Grey with a tiny amount of Skull White added in.*

Step 5. *Kornel painted the raised areas with a further highlight using the previous mix with a little more Skull White added in.*

Step 6. *A final highlight of pure Skull White was applied to the loincloth.*

Wing Membranes

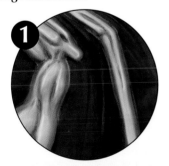

Step 1. *The wing membranes were basecoated with a 1:1 mix Liche Purple and Chaos Black.*

Step 2. *A highlight was made by adding in a little Kommando Khaki into the previous mix.*

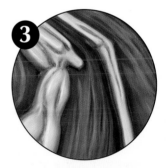

Step 3. *A second highlight was applied by adding in even more Kommando Khaki.*

Step 4. *The recesses beside the spars were shaded with Liche Purple with a small amount of Leviathan Purple added in.*

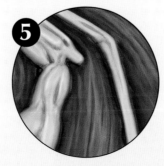

Step 5. *Kornel then applied a futher shade of watered-down Chaos Black into the recesses.*

Step 6. *Finally the membranes were highlighted by adding Kommando Khaki into the original basecoat mix.*

With the bulk of the Daemon Prince finished, Kornel had to complete the fine details across the model. He explained the theory that he'd used at this point:

'This is the stage in the painting of a miniature that people can often lose the overall effect of the miniature behind the details they are adding,' Kornel said. 'If you paint the minor elements in too striking a manner, they can overpower the whole model.' As an example he points out the cracked Space Marine helmet on the base.

'I wanted the base to have some extra details on it, but these couldn't dominate the model as a whole, so I chose the helmet from the Warhammer 40,000 Basing Kit. To stop it drawing too much attention, I painted it in dark tones to complement the armour plates of the Daemon Prince. Using the same armour style as the Daemon Prince means that the model is not tied into fighting against a specific foe. If it had been a Blood Angels or White Scars helmet it would have drawn the eye immediately to it, and also begged a whole range of questions when I want the Daemon Prince to be the sole focus of the piece.'

Looking at the finished model, Kornel has achieved his goal. All the details, from the pipes running through his flesh to the malign eye on his sword or even his horns, complement the model's colour scheme perfectly.

Cracked Helmet. *By using this small resin accessory from the Warhammer 40,000 Basing Kit, Kornel added a small, sympathetic detail to the model.*

Daemonic Blade. *Kornel used Kommando Khaki and Bleached Bone, washed with Baal Red, to paint the skulls and eye on the hilt of this sword. These colours tie it into the whole model.*

Metal Pipes. *These pipes brought a silver-metal touch to the miniature. Kornel used Chainmail as a basecoat and washed the pipes with a mix of Asurmen Blue and Badab Black.*

Horns. *Kornel used the horns to frame the Daemon Prince's face. They are dark at the tips and lighter towards the head, highlighted with the same colours as the Daemon's flesh.*

'EAVY METAL COLOUR FADES SHOWCASE

Daemon Princes are very well suited to utilising techniques such as colour fades, but they are far from the only miniatures that can benefit from this technique. Shown here are a handful of other models plucked from the 'Eavy Metal collection, each demonstrates how cunning use of colour fading can enhance a miniature and draw out the essential character of the model. Fantastical colours and the eerie way that one colour fades into another can often help to place a miniature in our worlds. Just look at how the sinister smoke drifts from the warpstone censer below or how the cloak of the Tainted gives off an inner light.

The muted shades of this Assassin's cloak suit a warrior that dwells in the shadows.

The Tainted has been painted so that a malign light seems to emanate from within.

Smooth colour fading on the Plague Priest's censer conveys the unnatural smoke perfectly.

Daemons of Tzeentch have skin that constantly flickers and shifts colour.

The Changeling's mercurial nature is emphasised by the fading colours on his robe.

The subtle colour fade on Sigvald the Magnificent's shield looks adds to his beauty.

DARK ELVES

WARHAMMER®

Neil Green is a veteran of the Masterclass series. Here he steps up to paint a Dark Elf Dreadlord mounted on Cold One. Expect sage advice about painting scales, armour and the pallid skin of the Dark Elves.

DREADLORD

There are many Dreadlords who owe their positions of power to their bloodlines, cruel and dashing exploits, or favour at Malekith's court. Others are granted temporary power by means of a writ of iron, granted by one of the rulers of the great cities of Naggaroth.

These Dreadlords are the leaders of the armies of Naggaroth, the generals of Malekith's war hosts and the captains of his ships. Ahead of mighty legions they sow terror and despair wherever they travel. Just like their liege lord, the Witch King, they have no pity in their hearts nor any concept of mercy. Instead their only desire is vengeance upon their unworthy kinsfolk on Ulthuan. Other races they disdain as beneath their attention, barely deserving of their concept and so they mete out suffering and slaughter upon them without hesistation. Thus the dread fleets of Naggaroth plunder the Old World and beyond with casual abandon – what do they care if ten thousand men die for them to accomplish their aims? To a Dreadlord it is no different to killing a dog.

A writ of iron grants the Dreadlord power and influence equal to that of his sponsor and control of mighty armies, but as ever in Naggarothi society, power is fleeting when ambitions flounder and defeat looms. Should a Dreadlord fail in his appointed task, the writ is melted down and the molten remains poured down the noble's throat. Such is the price of failure in Naggaroth.

Mike Anderson's brilliant Dreadlord, mounted on Jes Goodwin's distinctive Cold One, perfectly encapsulates the menace and power of a Dark Elf Noble. This made it was a wonderful candidate for a Masterclass. Once again, 'Eavy Metal veteran Neil Green volunteered to masterfully paint this beautiful miniature, offering to demonstrate the techniques of scales, armour and Elf flesh in detail.

Neil started by meticulously cleaning up all the components, before gluing them together with super glue. The fine joins were filled with green stuff and then filed down smooth when dry. The whole model was then undercoated Chaos Black.

The tail was painted with a dark basecoat, and then lighter colours were applied with a fine brush in lots of small, downward strokes.

The claws are also split into areas of scales and skin, and these were treated in the same way as the rest of the model.

It's always good to plan out your colour palette before you get started. For the Cold One, Neil wanted to use a palette of cold colours similar to the other Dark Elf Cold Ones, as a direct contrast to the warm reds that have been used for the Cold One mounts in the Lizardmen range.

Bearing that in mind, Neil went for a cool blue colour for the scales and then a complementary green for the creature's skin. When he was painting the skin, Neil thought the green was becoming too warm and so added Space Wolves Grey to the mix, as described in Step 3 below.

Painting the Skin

Step 1. For the Cold One's skin tones, Neil started with a basecoat of Orkhide Shade followed by a layer of Catachan Green.

Step 2. A 1:1 mix of Catachan Green and Camo Green was applied as a mid-tone. More Camo Green was added to the mix for the next layer.

Step 3. A highlight of Camo Green was then applied, followed by an even finer highlight using a 1:1 mix of Camo Green and Space Wolves Grey.

Step 4. The skin was given a wash of Asurmen Blue, and a final 1:3 highlight mix of Camo Green and Space Wolves Grey was applied to the most prominent areas.

Painting the Scales

Step 1. The scales were given a basecoat of Regal Blue. An initial 1:1 highlight mix of Regal Blue and Rotting Flesh was applied to the edges of each of the scales.

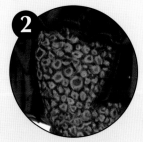

Step 2. A further highlight layer was applied, adding a bit more Rotting Flesh to the mix before painting it onto the edges of the scales once more.

Step 3. A wash of Asurmen Blue and Thraka Green was applied all over the scales. The highlight mix was then reapplied, followed by a wash of Thraka Green.

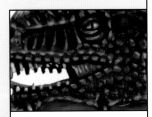

Other Scale Colours

The 'Eavy Metal team have also painted some Dark Elf Cold Ones in ruddy dark greens, highlighting them with white and yellow.

Dark blues and deep purples have been associated with every incarnation of Dark Elves we've produced over the years. Traditionally, purple is also linked with nobility because it was an expensive dye that only the rich could afford. So, for the Dreadlord, Neil wanted it to be the prominent colour. It also contrasts well against the cool blue and green of the Cold One. To get a rich, deep purple, Neil used a base of Liche Purple with a shade mixed from Chaos Black and Liche Purple.

The shield was painted using the same method as the purple cloth, although Neil added far starker highlighting to the sharp edges of the shield.

Purple Cloth

Step 1. The cloth was given a basecoat of Liche Purple. A 1:1 mix of Liche Purple and Chaos Black was then painted into the recessed areas.

Step 2. An initial highlight using a 2:1:1 mix of Liche Purple, Warlock Purple and Bleached Bone was painted onto all but the deepest recesses.

Step 3. Three further highlights were added, each time with a bit more Bleached Bone in the mix. A wash of a 2:1:1 mix of Liche Purple, Warlock Purple and Chaos Black was then applied to the whole area.

Step 4. For the final stage, the raised areas of the cloth were once again highlighted, this time with a 1:1:2 mix of Liche Purple, Warlock Purple and Bleached Bone.

Painting Skin

Step 1. A basecoat of pure Vermin Brown was painted on, followed by a 1:1 mix of Vermin Brown and Dwarf Flesh.

Step 2. A layer of Dwarf Flesh was then brushed on to the raised areas of the face, followed by a 3:1 mix of Dwarf Flesh and Bleached Bone.

Step 3. A highlight of a 1:1 mix of Dwarf Flesh and Bleached Bone was then used. A further highlight was applied, adding a little Skull White to the mix.

Step 4. The eyes were painted with Scorched Brown and "dotted" with Bleached Bone. The face was shaded with watered down Scorched Brown.

Another example of planning out your colours before you begin painting can be seen on the Cold One. Both silver and gold were used on the armour to highlight the fact that this Cold One was a Dreadlord's mount. The Cold One's armoured helm, the champron, was painted gold to suggest a crown, further defining the mount as one of the largest and most vicious examples of the species. The chainmail on both the Dreadlord's legs and the Cold One's barding was edged with gold. On the Dreadlord himself, gold banding was used on his armour, again to mark him out as a character and make him stand out when placed in the ranks of the Cold One Knights.

Painting Steel

Step 1. Neil started by painting a basecoat of Boltgun Metal all over the metal areas.

Step 2. Next he shaded the metal with a thinned-down 1:1 mix of Chaos Black and Codex Grey. The Boltgun Metal was reapplied, followed by a highlight of Chainmail.

Step 3. A wash of Devlan Mud was added next. When this was dry, the areas were washed again with Badab Black. Finally, the raised areas and edges were highlighted with Mithril Silver.

Painting Gold

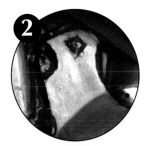

Step 1. A 1:1 mix of Shining Gold and Scorched Brown was used as a basecolour. When dry, Neil washed the area with watered-down Scorched Brown.

Step 2. Shining Gold was brushed on over the basecoat, followed by a highlight using a 1:1 mix of Shining Gold and Mithril Silver.

Step 3. A wash of Devlan Mud was then applied, before a final wash of Gryphonne Sepia was used to finish off the gold effect.

Gold Inlay

'Eavy Metal's Joe Tomaszewski took a different approach to the armour of his Dreadlord, and gave the model a really ostentatious look by using a gold inlay. First he painted the metal areas silver, and then he marked off the gold areas with Chaos Black. These were then painted with the gold method used by Neil. The silver areas were then re-highlighted where they met the gold banding.

The shield design was painted by Neil in freehand. It does take a bit of practice to be able to paint glyphs, sigils and other race markings with just a brush and a steady hand, but even the guys in 'Eavy Metal don't always get it right on their first attempt. To start with it's always best to draw your design on a piece of paper and then copy it. Don't

make it up on the fly – it rarely works! Spacing and size are also very important; use dots to mark prominent points or some other visual cue to make sure your design fits into the space. Take your time and draw the basic shape, even if it's quite rough at first. The joy of painting means you can always cover up any mistakes and refine your design.

Battle Standard

Joe converted his Dreadlord into a Battle Standard Bearer with a simple weapon swap for the standard. As you can see from the picture above, the banner itself features an icon designed by Joe and painted on freehand. For Joe it was important that the design was placed in the middle of the banner, so he carefully plotted the centre and extreme points of the icon before he started painting it.

Painting Black

Step 1. Starting with a Chaos Black basecoat, Neil highlighted it with a 1:1 mix of Chaos Black and Codex Grey, and then applied a further highlight of Codex Grey.

Step 2. A further highlight of Fortress Grey was then lightly applied, before being shaded with a wash of Badab Black.

Step 3. When dry, Neil reapplied Fortress Grey highlights. A final highlight of a 1:1 mix of Fortress Grey and Skull White was then added to the most raised areas.

Painting the Shield Rune

Step 1. Once Neil had finalised a design, he copied it very carefully onto the surface of the shield with Vomit Brown.

Step 2. Bleached Bone was used to create a fine keyline around the edge of the design.

Step 3. Neil then carefully tidied up the design using Skull White and Liche Purple to further define and neaten up the image.

Final Details

To finish the model Neil picked out the smaller details, such as the Cold One's eye, the rune at the base of the sword blade and the skulls.

While it's tempting to rush through these last few bits, you should always spend plenty of time on them to make sure the whole model comes together.

The eye was painted using a mix of Vomit Brown and Bleached Bone. A black slit was carefully painted in the centre of the eye.

The teeth and claws were given a basecoat of Vomit Brown, followed by a midtone of Bleached Bone and a highlight of Skull White.

The skulls were first painted using Graveyard Earth, then a 1:1 mix of Graveyard Earth and Bleached Bone, followed by a Skull White highlight.

The icon on the Cold One's skull was carefully painted on using a 1:1 mix of Regal Blue and Chaos Black.

DISPLAY MODELS

Here we look at Joe Tomaszweski's Chaos Lord, the 2009 Games Day-exclusive miniature, painted with jaw-dropping non-metallic metal. Read on to see how he accomplished this impressive feat.

CHAOS LORD

Every year Games Workshop holds a number of Games Day events around the world – these are the most iconic and exciting events on the hobby calendar. From the United States to Germany, each is a celebration of gaming and painting and on attendance you're surrounded by so many great-looking games and miniatures that it's hard not to feel the excitement.

On of the things that many attendees get very excited about each year is the Games Day miniature – each is a masterpiece, sculpted by a Citadel miniatures designer for the pure joy of creating a fantastic model. These quickly become collectors pieces, finding places in display cabinets, armies and memory boxes across the globe.

In 2009 the Games Day-exclusive miniature was sculpted by Martin Footit. It was a mighty Chaos Lord, gripping paired axes in its mighty fists. Replete with details that set him apart as a champion of the Dark Gods, this model is a sensational candidate for a Masterclass.

'Eavy Metal's Joe Tomaszewski stepped forward to do the honours, with the promise that he would really go to town on the model. Joe saw this as an exquisite display model, something for show rather than the rigours of gaming.

With this in mind, Joe wanted to give the model a scenic base to make it even more imposing and paint it in a very advanced technique that is particularly suitable for displaying miniatures. The technique is non-metallic metal. This is challenging to achieve but in the hands of an 'Eavy Metal painter the finished effect will be stunning. That's not to say you have to be an expert to give it a go, far from it!

Over the following pages we'll show and explain exactly how Joe achieved the armour effect, including some detailed instructions and guidelines on exactly how the theory behind non-metallic metal works. By following these tips, along with the step-by-steps guidelines (and with some hard work and practice) you'll be able to replicate the effects on your own models.

Scenic Base

The base was taken from a small glass jar lid that was sprayed black. Slate was then glued on it to create a stepped pile. For further texture a lone skull was stuck on and some Green Stuff used to fill in the unsightly gaps.

When painting a model purely for display you should always consider the direction from which the model will be viewed. This is not only to position the model in the best aspect but will also have a factor on how light sources will play off and reflect onto a model. This is especially important when painting in a non-metallic metal scheme, as incorrectly judging how the light works could compromise the paint job. In this case Joe wanted the model to be viewed straight on so he highlighted and shaded the armour to reflect that.

Once the armour was fully painted, Joe used coloured glazes to give it an almost unearthly hue.

Painting Metal Without Metallics

Step 1. After undercoating the entire model Chaos Black, Joe began by basecoating the armour plates with Codex Grey.

Step 2. Watered-down Chaos Black was applied as a rough, heavy wash around the joins and raised areas of the armour.

Step 3. After the wash, Codex Grey was applied again to the raised areas to neaten up and form the basis of the highlight stages.

Step 4. A 2:1 mix of Codex Grey and Skull White was next, finely applied along the angle lines of the armour plates.

Step 5. For the next layer the mix was reversed, so it was a 2:1 mix of Skull White and Codex Grey, again working up the highlight lines already established.

Step 6. Dots of pure Skull White were then applied at points where the highlight lines met to represent points of direct reflection.

Glazing the Armour

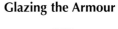

Step 1. A glaze, made from watered-down Liche Purple, was applied around the bottom portions of the armour plates.

Step 2. A light glaze using Hawk Turquoise overlaid this. It's a very subtle layer but gives the armour an arcane quality.

The chain mail was simply painted black, and then Codex Grey was applied to the bottom of the links, which was in turn highlighted with Skull White.

The fur was basecoated Astronomican Grey and then given a wash using a 1:1 mix of Hawk Turquoise and Chaos Black. It was highlighted back up to Astronomican Grey, and then highlighted further with Skull White.

When you paint horns you can go from dark at the base and lighter at the tip, or shade in the opposite direction, having a lighter base and darkening at the top. Either method can be effective and depends on your style and the model itself. For this project Joe has chosen to lighten the base of the horns. This is because, bearing in mind it's a display model, he wants the eyes of the spectator to be drawn towards the face – the lightest part of the model.

This is just one of the tricks an experienced painter can use to grab the viewer's attention and subconsciously draw their eyes to parts of the model they want the spectator to acknowledge first, before they appraise the entire model.

Painting the Shield

Step 1. The shield was first painted using a 1:1 mix of Codex Grey and Chaos Black. Joe painted carefully around the accoutrements hanging from the shield.

Step 2. Pure Codex Grey was built up in many thin layers vertically along the shield's curvature. A thin outline of Codex Grey was also applied to the shield's edge.

Step 3. Fortress Grey was then applied over the same areas in the previous step. Thin layers carefully blending with the previous coat of paint is the key.

Step 4. Skull White was used to add nuanced highlights on the shield, applied mainly along the edges but also to create tiny 'scratches' on the surface.

Painting the Horns

Step 1. Snakebite Leather was applied as thin stripes along the length of the horns; brush control is needed to keep the stripes separate and neat.

Step 2. Next, Bleached Bone was overlaid along the Snakebite Leather stripes, tapering out towards the tips.

Step 3. Skull White was then added in thin layers over the Bleached Bone stripes, keeping the majority of the layers close to the base of the four horns.

Step 4. Joe then added chips with carefully applied Chaos Black and Skull White. Finally, a thin wash of Chaos Black was brushed over the ends of the horns.

NON-METALLIC METAL

The process known as non-metallic metal is a technique that uses paints without metallic pigments to create reflective, mostly metal-looking surfaces. Shades and highlights are created in a pictorial fashion using the same methods that artists have been doing on canvas for centuries. In effect, you're using a two dimensional technique on a three dimensional model. That's quite a challenging prospect and for this reason painting with non-metallic metal is a very advanced technique that requires mastery of many other expert techniques, such as rich blending and advanced colour theory. Nevertheless, the 'Eavy Metal team get asked a lot about how to achieve such an effect and so we'll attempt to cover the basics here. Whilst reading this page will give you some foundation in the technique, practice and solid brush control are the keys to getting this effect right.

Models painted up in non-metallic metals are primarily for display. It's rarely used on models intended for use in the gaming environment where the chance of such a precisely painted model being chipped is much higher. The best way to showcase a miniature with non-metallic metal painting is in a lighted display cabinet, where the dedicated spotlights accentuate the exaggerations painted onto the model. Considering where the light shines upon the model and how it reflects off surfaces is actually a good place to start.

Light Sourcing

Metallic objects reflect light differently to other surfaces and this needs to be exaggerated when applying paint to a miniature. On metallic objects light dramatically changes from dark to light when the surface changes shape. So to achieve the non-metallic metal effect you need to imagine, or even draw a plan, where your light points are around the model so you can place your highlights and shade. Four points of light around a figure are generally best; you then plot how each area of non-metallic metal will react according to where the light points are on the miniature. The geometric diagrams on this page illustrate how light reflects off different shapes.

When he painted his Harry the Hammer, Darren Latham imagined four light sources around the miniature. This helped him visualise where the highlights and shades should be.

Illustrations, from fantasy art in particular, also show how artists achieve reflective surfaces in two-dimensional form. In this case real world references are not very useful, as they don't convey the exaggerated highlighting and shading you need to make the technique effective. Following a real-world reference will just leave you with a drab grey or yellow area rather than the metallic-look you're trying to achieve.

Left. Dave Gallagher's illustration is a perfect example of how artists paint metal in two-dimensional form.

Below. A graphical representation of how light falls on simple geometric shapes, giving you a rough guide about how to add highlights and shading to your non-metallic metals.

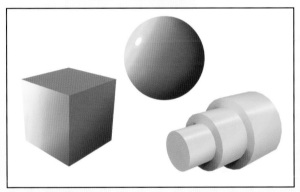

Contrast

When paining non-metallic metal, contrast is the key. Each surface needs to go from black to white. Normally you highlight with a lighter version of the midtone. So for, say, Regal Blue, you might highlight with Enchanted Blue. However, when painting in a non-metallic metal technique you should always shade and highlight with black and white no matter what the midtone is.

The other facet to this process is that you should add colour to the surface to bring it to life. Metal surfaces reflect the environment around them so, if the model is meant to be in a cave, your colour scheme will not be as bright as a miniature in strong daylight. The contrast, coupled with adding 'light spots' (bearing in mind where your light points are on the model), will exaggerate the reflective quality of the metal. When you actually apply the paint you must do it in thin layers and then create a seamless blend, starting with the midtone and shading down and before highlighting up.

Have a Go

These are just guidelines, the real results will come from practice and learning the theory. Don't forget artists have been doing this for years in pictures so take inspiration from them and don't be afraid to just give it a go.

The bandages were painted with Dheneb Stone followed by a Baal Red and Devlan Mud wash. The area was then highlighted with Dheneb Stone, with a final highlight of Skull White.

The loincloth started with a Regal Blue basecoat, which had Scab Red slowly blended into it for the first highlights. It was then highlighted with Kommando Khaki, before Skull White was added to the mix for a final, layered highlight.

A lot of Joe's methods involve starting with a basecoat midtone, then shading down with a wash, before lightening back up to the midtone and beyond to the highlight colour. Joe does it this way because it gives him a smoother blend between layers, and it's easier than painstakingly blending to a darker shade. Another good tip is, when using a colour like khaki to highlight a multi-coloured area such as the cloak, you should mix the highlight with the colour on the lower layer, rather than straight across. So, in the case of the cloak, the khaki highlight was blended with Regal Blue and then Scab Red as Joe worked the highlights to the edge.

Painting the Inner Cloak

Step 1. The lining of the cloak was first given a basecoat of Astronomican Grey. This was a solid layer that covered the entire area of the cloak lining.

Step 2. Separate washes of Regal Blue, Liche Purple and Chaos Black were painted into the recessed areas. Joe randomly applied each colour wash.

Step 3. Joe then worked up the raised areas back to Astronomican Grey, this was followed by a 1:1 mix of Skull White and Astronomican Grey.

Step 4. A final strong highlight layer of Skull White was then applied to finish off the cloak. This was built up over many thin layers.

Painting the Outer Cloak

Step 1. The outside of the cloak was first basecoated with a solid coat of Regal Blue.

Step 2. Starting with the Regal Blue, Joe added Scab Red to the mix, slowly and consistently adding more with each layer until he had blended to pure Scab Red.

Step 3. The recesses and deep folds of the cloak were shaded with a wash of Chaos Black.

Step 4. The cloak was highlighted with Kommando Khaki, mixed with each colour it covered. This was then given a final highlight of Skull White.

The intricate freehand design on the axe head was replicated on both the axes and across various parts of the Chaos Lord's armour.

The skulls were painted using a very similar method to the bandages, the only difference being the wash, which was pure Devlan Mud instead of Baal Red.

To really showcase his astounding skills Joe has added some freehand design onto the Chaos Warrior's armour and weapons. Applying an intricate design onto a surface you' ve already spent hours painting to look like shining magical armour is not for the faint-hearted! Freehand designs are usually painted onto a neutral surface, something that can easily be painted over if a mistake is made, but obviously Joe didn't have that luxury here. He first drew his design on paper and then slowly and accurately translated it onto the figure's armour and weapons. We can only recommend patience and pinpoint accuracy with a brush if you try this yourself.

Painting the Gold Leaf

Step 1. Joe's non-metallic gold leaf starts with a basecoat of Snakebite Leather. A thin line of Chaos Black was used to enhance and separate the design from it's surroundings.

Step 2. The Snakebite Leather was then shaded with a very thin wash of Chaos Black.

Step 3. Joe started to build up the design using a mix of Snakebite Leather and Skull White, adding more white into the mix over several layers.

Step 4. Skull White was used to edge the design. This was divided from the design with a thin line of Codex Grey, creating the impression of a silver edge.

Painting the Helmet

Step 1. The helmet was painted in a similar method to the gold leaf, starting with a basecoat of Snakebite Leather.

Step 2. This was followed by a shade into the recesses with a wash of Chaos Black.

Step 3. The Snakebite midtone was reapplied and then worked up by adding an increasing amount of Skull White over several layers.

Step 4. Pure Skull White was applied to the raised areas, and purple and turquoise glazes were used to achieve the same subtle effect as the armour.

The pendant was painted using the same technique that Joe used for the Chaos Lord's golden helm.

The shield straps were painted in a simple three-stage method: a base of Scorched Brown, followed by a layer of Vermin Brown and then Bleached Bone.

The axe haft was given a base colour of Scorched Brown. Joe mixed this colour with Bleached Bone, painting on the wood grain in progressively lighter mixes.

The pouch was painted Astronomican Grey and then given a Badab Black wash. The Astronomican Grey was reapplied and then highlighted with pure Skull White.

'EAVY METAL SHOWCASE

A selection of Chaos Warriors.

Vampire Lord

Skeleton Warrior

Wood Elf Spellsinger

Greatsword standard bearer

Skaven Clanrat

Skaven Slave

Orc Boyz

Bloodcrusher of Khorne

Saurus Temple Guard

MORDOR TROLL

THE LORD OF THE RINGS
STRATEGY BATTLE GAME

The multi-part plastic Troll Kit provides painters with the opportunity to hone their skills with scales, armour and monstrous flesh. Expert painter Fil Dunn is on hand to talk us through how to paint a fearsome Mordor Troll.

The Trolls of Mordor are dire creations wrought by the diabolical hand of Sauron. Rumours and deceptions abound as to their unnatural origins, but the reality of their presence renders such speculation shockingly impertinent.

Mordor Trolls loom over the Dark Lord's throngs, standing twice the height of a Orc, even the stronger, taller Orcs who guard the Morannon. They wield massive clubs or swords, great hunks of wood and metal that can cut a horse in twain with a single blow or crush through both armour and shield with sickening force.

Entire legions of Mordor Trolls guard the Morannon, that Black Gate that bars the entry into the Dark Lord's domain, a powerful force that spells doom to any who would oppose them. Others are spread throughout the legions of Mordor, doing the bidding of Sauron's captains with dogged, if somewhat simplistic determination. These are the most commonly sighted, and those greatest feared, for a rabble of Orcs might be considered small threat until they bring the crushing bulk of a Troll to bear. Against such fury shield walls buckle and resolve

shatters – for what man can hope to stand against an avalanche of muscle and rage dredged up from their worst nightmares?

Amongst any collection of The Lord of the Rings models a Mordor Troll has the opportunity to stand out as a centrepiece, providing aspiring painters with a canvas onto which they can express their skill. As such it would be a shame not to expend a great deal of time and effort when painting it for your collection so that you can make it look as great as it can be.

Step forward 'Eavy Metal painter Fil Dunn, the man with the brush skills to take the Troll miniature from the bare grey plastic of the frame and onto the battlefield looking spectacular in glorious colour.

Fil started the project by detaching all of the plastic components from the frame using the Citadel Plastic Cutters and Hobby Knife. He then cleaned up all of the parts with the knife and files, before sticking the kit together as a Mordor Troll. When the plastic glue had dried, Fil gave the entire model an undercoat of Chaos Black. He used several thin coats of Chaos Black spray paint, before touching it up with Chaos Black from the pot.

A purple glaze was applied to the skin around the eye sockets to make the face slightly paler than the rest of the Troll's flesh.

For the Troll's skin, Fil chose quite a pale tone to make a very deliberate contrast to the dark tarnished armour and leathers he planned to paint later. Fil painted the flesh with a lined, loose-looking texture, mimicking the skin of large mammals such as rhinos and elephants for the Troll's flesh. Larger animals tend to have loose, sagging skin compared to smaller creatures. By replicating this look on the Troll flesh, Fil intended to create a sense of scale. As ever, the Internet is useful for finding reference material, as are encyclopaedias or natural history books that contain good, high-quality photographs. Don't be afraid to use real-world references when painting miniatures.

Painting the Skin

Step 1. To start with, Fil blocked in all of the flesh areas of the Mordor Troll with an even basecoat of Scorched Brown.

Step 2. For the next stage he started to build up the skin with a 1:1 mix of Scorched Brown and Tallarn Flesh, applying the paint across the flesh in horizontal lines.

Step 3. Next, Fil used a coat of pure Tallarn Flesh, applying it as before to give a wrinkled appearance to the skin.

Step 4. A 1:1 mix of Tallarn Flesh and Dwarf Flesh was then applied to the flesh of the model brushed on in lines across the body, adding to the appearance of the creases.

Step 5. Next, a 1:1:1 mix of Tallarn Flesh, Dwarf Flesh and Bleached Bone was used. Fil continued to apply the paint across the same areas to keep the dark furrows.

Step 6. To finish the skin, a glaze was applied to the whole area using a 1:1:1 mix of Matt Varnish, Ogryn Flesh and Leviathan Purple.

Working Inside Out

When painting a model of any size, Fil works from the inside out, first painting the skin, then the cloth, the armour and other outer accoutrements. This way he doesn't have to worry too much about being messy on the earlier layers because he'll get to the outer layers later and can tidy up any stray paint strokes by painting over the top of them.

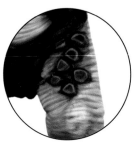

Fil lined in the area around the scales using Scorched Brown rather than Chaos Black, which would have been too stark.

We refer to the rough patches of skin found on the Troll's legs and back as scales for the purpose of this painting feature. This is because they are painted using the exact same method as the scales you'll find on our Dragons, Cold Ones or any number of the creatures found in a Warhammer Lizardmen army.

The 'Eavy Metal team use a similar method for painting scales no matter which creature it is – a basecoat, a wash, followed by two highlights. Fil used a basecoat of Scorched Brown for these scales. Scorched Brown was used repeatedly across the whole model – for the skin, the scales and the leather – tying the colour palette together.

Soft and Hard Highlights

When painting a monster it can be difficult to decide on the best way to apply highlights. Adding a very severe highlight will not always work. A good rule of thumb is that if it is a "gloss" surface, like a claw, shiny chitinous plates, scales or teeth, then the highlight can be quite harsh. If you're highlighting a matt surface, like skin or cloth, which diffuses light rather than reflects it, then a much softer highlight should be used instead.

Painting the Scales

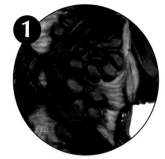

Step 1. The scales were first basecoated with Scorched Brown. The basecoat was applied both to the scales themselves and the area of skin around them.

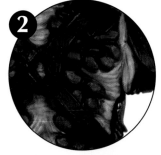

Step 2. A dark brown wash of Devlan Mud was then liberally applied over the top of the basecoat. Fil made sure it covered the entire area, knowing that you can be generous with the washes without affecting the tone.

Step 3. The first highlight applied was a 1:1 mix of Scorched Brown and Bleached Bone. Fil carefully applied this mix to the edge of each separate scale.

Step 4. For the last stage, a sharp highlight was applied to the most prominent edges of the scales, adding some more Bleached Bone to the previous mix.

The sword was painted in the same way as the armour, but Fil used only a couple of wash layers, making the overall effect brighter.

The helmet uses the same method as the armour. You can see the the watered-down Vermin Brown wash, which represents rust forming in the recesses.

When painting armour, Fil likes to create dark metal tones, before adding brighter highlights to create a very strong contrast. This is further complemented by the Troll's pale skin colour.

A very dark, almost black, iron-like colour works on evil creatures such as Orcs and Trolls really well, as the darker the metal, the more tarnished and ill-kempt it looks.

When painting dark metal, it's important to create an extreme highlight along the edges to create a strong contrast and help delineate the outline of the armour. This is best seen with the helmet as shown in the inset above. All metal areas of the model were painted in the same way.

Painting the Breastplate

Step 1. All the metal areas of the Troll were painted with a basecoat of Boltgun Metal. Boltgun Metal tends to be quite thick, so make sure you keep it fluid by adding water.

Step 2. For the next stage the breastplate was given six layers of Badab Black wash, taking the shine off the Boltgun Metal. Make sure each layer of wash is dry before applying the next.

Step 3. Fil used a fine brush to carefully apply the paint chips and scratches with Mithril Silver. The armour edging was also given an extreme highlight of Mithril Silver at the same time.

Step 4. A wash of Badab Black was applied to some of the chips to age them. A final wash of Vermin Brown was added to create a rusty look to parts of the armour, especially in the recesses.

Metal Chips

There are many ways of painting chips and dents in metal armour. One extreme method used on metal models is to score the painted armour with a knife to expose the actual metal underneath. Fil created his chips and flecks with Mithril Silver and a steady hand. He applied a wash of Badab Black to some of the chips (but not all) to age the armour and make it look as though the damage has happened over time rather than all at once.

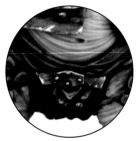

The Troll's loin cloth was painted in the same way as the black hide, with a brown leather belt and metal clasp.

The strap ring was painted with Boltgun Metal. A small amount of Devlan Mud has been applied around the metal studs of the strap.

The Troll is wearing two types of leather – the straps are painted in a traditional brown colour and the hide that the Troll is wearing underneath the armour is much darker, almost black. Even though both types of leather have different colourations, the basecolour of both is Scorched Brown, as used in both the Troll's scales and skin.

As with the armour, Fil wanted to keep the leather dark to contrast with the paleness of the skin and the bright edging highlight of the metallic areas. It's always good to plan ahead when painting a centrepiece model like this, so you can think about colour theory and the effects of contrast and balance across the whole of a miniature.

Aged Leather

To make the leather look more realistic, Fil applied highlights to age it. As leather is a readily available material, finding a suitable reference shouldn't be a problem. Studying items like old leather belts and black leather jackets can give you a good idea of how leather wears and cracks.

For the straps, Fil highlighted fine cracks along the edge that work their way into the centre, around the areas that would realistically incur the most movement, such as around the shoulders.

Painting Leathers

Step 1. *The black leather was given a 1:1 basecoat mix of Chaos Black and Scorched Brown. The straps were basecoated with pure Scorched Brown.*

Step 2. *The black leather was then shaded with watered-down Chaos Black, although you could also use Badab Black. Fil then gave the straps a wash of Devlan Mud.*

Step 3. *A highlight using a 1:1 mix of Scorched Brown and Bleached Bone was applied to the raised areas of the black leather. A Bestial Brown highlight was also painted onto the very edge of the straps.*

Step 4. *More Bleached Bone was added to the previous mix for a final highlight on the black leather. Snakebite Leather was used to create creases and cracks in the leather straps as described in the box on the left.*

Final Details

The Troll's sword was made to look bloody with layers of Scorched Brown, Scab Red and then Blood Red, followed by a wash of Devlan Mud. The final layer is a 1:1 mix of Blood Red and Gloss Varnish to give it that glistening, visceral look.

The Troll's nails were painted with Scorched Brown. The lines were painted with Graveyard Earth and then Fortress Grey. A wash of Gryphonne Sepia was then applied, followed by a final highlight of Bleached Bone.

The severed head on the Troll's harness was painted with the same mix of paint as the Troll flesh, with a bit of Fortress Grey added.

The finished Mordor Troll, complete with a scenic base.

Fil blocked in the eyes with Chaos Black and then added a tiny highlight of Skull White.

You can assemble your plastic Troll in a variety of different ways, such as those shown here.

THE SANGUINOR

WARHAMMER 40,000

In this masterclass Darren Latham unleashes his talents to demonstrate non-metallic metal techniques, tackling the striking golden armour of the Blood Angels most beatific hero, the Sanguinor.

The Sanguinor is a hero of the Blood Angels Chapter, a gold-armoured champion whose actions and origins remain a mystery.

While none can prove the origins of the Sanguinor, any Blood Angels Space Marine will affirm that he is a shining angel of vengeance, a hero who fights alongside the Chapter when their need is direst. Whether his arrival is witnessed by only a handful of Battle-Brothers, whose fight for survival is aided by their golden-armoured saviour, or an entire strike force consisting of multiple battle companies, the result is the same. From the moment he arrives upon the field of battle, the Sanguinor is a whirlwind of righteous violence, his Glaive Encarmine lopping off heads and limbs with each masterful stroke.

This unusual and action-packed background makes the Sanguinor something of an enigma for those of us

who relish the chance to delve into the grim darkness of the Warhammer 40,000 galaxy. Though many, even those within the Imperium itself, question his existence and his motives, the Blood Angels, and those his actions have saved from calamity, know better.

For 'Eavy Metal's Darren Latham, tackling the Sanguinor miniature presented a chance to go to town with an extraordinary paint job. 'This figure lends itself to non-metallic metal painting,' Darren explains. 'A golden-armoured hero such as this, with his huge unfurled wings, will really stand out amongst the sea of red and black power armour found amongst the rest of the Studio's Blood Angels army. The model is so resonant of Sanguinius, and using non-metallic colours to paint the gold will help the Sanguinor to catch the eye whenever he's on the tabletop, even as part of massive battle shot.'

Painting Non-metallic Metals

It's clear sitting down with Darren that he really thought long and hard about how best to paint the Sanguinor. 'The Sanguinor model is a painter's delight,' he says. 'Look at all the detail, the musculature on his stomach and the features of the face mask he wears. A model like this offers a chance to really show what a skilled painter can do with non-metallic metals.' Earlier in this book Joe Tomazewski did a non-metallic metal Masterclass of a Chaos Warrior clad in silver metal – check it out for an in-depth look at the theory behind this technique. 'Painting non-metallic gold, while it uses the same principles, is quite different. Non-metallic gold has lots of colours, such as yellows and browns, in it.'

Why use non-metallic metal at all, though, is the question on the minds of many? 'The joy of painting with this technique is the illusion that you've painted the model gold,' Darren says. 'It's a real challenge to do it, and do a fantastic Citadel miniature, with all its shapes, folds and lines justice at the same time.'

Darren's also keen to point out that non-metallic metal isn't the only way to get a beautiful metallic effect on a Citadel miniature. 'Oh no,' he explains. 'The Citadel Colour range includes plenty of metallic colours and they are the staple of any 'Eavy Metal painter's palette when we normally paint metal on a miniature – but sometimes we want to make a model stand out and so employ our skills to the fullest. The opportunity to paint a model as exciting and detailed as the Sanguinor brings out the best painter in all of us.'

Looking at the Studio's Blood Angels army you can see what Darren means. Most of the gold armour in the army has been painted using Shining Gold and the other metallic Citadel paints, as you can see in the feature earlier in the issue. 'Painters shouldn't be put off from using metallic colours,' Darren emphasises. 'Painting with metallics can be just as rewarding, and equally as impressive. I've every intention of painting a second Sanguinor for just that reason,' he says.

Metallic and Non-metallic Comparison

Commander Dante in metallic (left) and non-metallic (right) metals

Captain Tycho in metallic (left) and non-metallic (right) metals

Sanguinary Guard in metallic (top) and non-metallic (bottom) metals

Most of the Sanguinor miniature is painted gold. Because he wanted a dark starting point, Darren undercoated the model with Chaos Black Spray.

Darren blended each consecutive layer by keeping his paints thin and being careful not to paint over the previous layer entirely.

Step 1. The armour was basecoated with a 1:1 mix of Calthan Brown and Snakebite Leather. If you paint 'out of the lines' while doing the armour, don't worry – there'll be time to clean up later.

Step 2. Next Darren added the first layer of blending – he used a mix of Snakebite Leather with a spot of Bleached Bone, painted onto the areas where the light source would be reflecting from the model.

Step 3. More Bleached Bone was added to the previous mix, bringing the proportions to about 2:1 Snakebite Leather to Bleached Bone.

Step 4. Again, Darren added a little more Bleached Bone into the earlier mix, this time bringing the quantities to 1:1. This was then watered down and painted on, blending into the earlier stages.

Step 5. For the fifth stage, yet more Bleached Bone was added to the brown mix from Step 4 (the ratio at this point was roughly 1:2 Snakebite Leather to Bleached Bone).

Step 6. Next, watered-down Dark Flesh was washed into the recesses. The effect is to subtly enrich the recessed areas. Darren added flat shading above the highlights, creating artificial reflection.

Step 7. Darren then mixed Chaos Black with Dark Flesh (1:2) before watering it down. As before this was carefully painted into the recesses and above the lighter areas to create the impression of reflection.

Step 8. In this stage a further highlight, this time of pure watered-down Bleached Bone, was painted on. This is quite an extreme highlight, and is painted on the points where the reflection of the light is sharpest.

Step 9. Darren added a further shade of watered-down Chaos Black. It's important to keep this shade very tight and fine, so as not to overpower the ones you have already added.

Step 10. In stark contrast to the black shading applied in Stage 9, an extreme highlight of Skull White was applied very sparingly. Note the spots added at the points of direct reflection.

Step 11. Next Darren added a wash of watered-down Sunburst Yellow. This was applied over all of the armour, to accentuate the gold colours. Once dry he followed it with with a glaze of Leviathan Purple into the recesses.

Step 12. Finally, Darren re-applied the most extreme of the Skull White highlights – this starkly contrasts with the yellow hue of the other highlights, creating the impression of bright light reflecting.

Finished Armour

Here you can see the completed armour and jump pack, showing how Darren has applied the non-metallic metal across the whole model. With the armour completed, Darren pressed on to add the extra details, which we'll explain later. Because the armour is the main part of the model, Darren completed it before moving on to the other areas of the miniature – whichever way round you approach it, you run the risk of painting over something you have already finished. Darren always paints the largest area first, reasoning that he'll be using more detailed brushes later (and thus be less likely to make mistakes). For those of us who aren't talented to the same degree as 'Eavy Metal, however, it's all a matter of confidence, practice and correcting mistakes when we make them.

Models shown slightly larger than actual size.

Chalice

The Sanguinor clasps a powerful Glaive Encarmine in one hand and an ornate chalice in the other – while the first is a powerful close combat weapon, the other is a deeply symbolic representation of the Chapter's history and heritage. Darren painted these using subtle colours, so as to keep the focal point on the Sanguinor himself.

Step 1. Darren started the chalice by painting it with a smooth basecoat of Adeptus Battlegrey.

Step 2. Next, a highlight of Codex Grey was applied, focusing on the areas where light would reflect from the chalice.

Step 3. A further highlight of Fortress Grey followed next. Again, Darren made sure to focus on how light would reflect from the chalice.

Step 4. The recesses of the chalice were shaded by painting on a 1:1:1 mix of Regal Blue, Chaos Black and Codex Grey.

Step 5. Darren then added a darker shade to the recesses, this time with watered-down Chaos Black paint.

Step 6. Finally Darren singled out the extreme highlights, using Skull White to pick out the areas where the reflection of light was strongest.

Parchment

The Sanguinor model has impressive parchments that drape from his waist. Darren painted these using Khemri Brown as a basecoat, which he then highlighted by adding in increasing amounts of Dheneb Stone. He washed the recesses with a 1:1 mix of Scorched Brown and Badab Black, followed by a second wash of pure Gryphonne Sepia.

The purity seals were painted with a mix of Chaos Black and Scab Red, which was highlighted with Scab Red with a little Bleached Bone mixed into successive highlights, before a final touch of pure Bleached Bone.

Darren then carefully detailed the parchment by painting on miniscule text and Imperial iconography, including the aquila and Blood Angels Chapter symbol.

Jewels and Gems

Like many Blood Angels, the Sanguinor is decorated with a number of gem stones. Darren used the following technique to create give the gems their realistic appearance.

Step 1. Darren painted the whole gemstone in the colour of your choice. When painting a gem, it pays to start with a fairly dark colour.

Step 2. Next, he painted a lighter colour onto the gem as a highlight – this highlight should be towards the light source.

Step 3. Darren added a further highlight within the first, this can be quite a stark highlight as you can see in the example on the right.

Step 4. Finally, he added spots of white to darker side, of the gem, creating the impression of light reflecting directly from the surface.

Angelic Wings and Glaive Encarmine

One of the most distinctive features of the Sanguinor are the bright, crisp and clean wings that stretch out from his back. In contrast to the parchment, which looks faded and age-worn, the wings are clean and white offering a strong contrast with the rest of the miniature. Here's how Darren painted them.

Angelic Wings

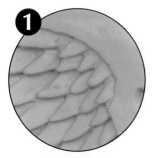

Step 1. *Darren started by applying a smooth basecoat to the wings, using a 1:2 mix of Fenris Grey and Astronomican Grey.*

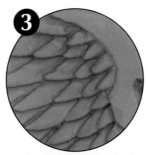

Step 2. *Next, Darren made a 1:1 mix of Codex Grey and Fenris Grey, which he watered-down and applied as a shading wash.*

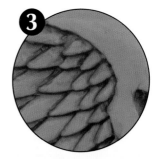

Step 3. *Chaos Black was added to the previous mix (equal parts of each) and painted into the very deepest recesses of the wings.*

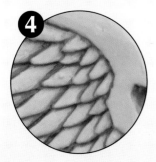

Step 4. *With the shading applied, Darren began adding highlights, first painting on a layer of Astronomican Grey.*

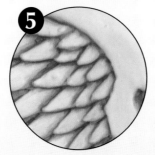

Step 5. *The next highlight was painted with a 1:1 mix of Skull White and Astronomican Grey – remember to keep the paint watered down.*

Step 6. *The final highlight is painted with pure Skull White – this is painted along the edges of the feather tips and the bend of the wings.*

Glaive Encarmine

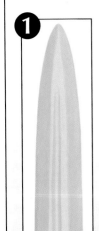

Step 1. *The sword was painted with a 1:1:1 mix of Regal Blue, Hawk Turqoise and Bleached Bone.*

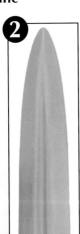

Step 2. *The whole blade was then highlighted by adding a little more Bleached Bone into the previous mix.*

Step 3. *For the second highlight, Darren added even more Bleached Bone and a little Skull White into the previous mix.*

Step 4. *Darren then shaded the centre of the blade's fullering with a 1:1 mix of Regal Blue and Hawk Turqoise.*

Step 5. *The fullering was then shaded with watered-down Chaos Black – it's important to keep this to the very centre, so go carefully as you paint.*

Step 6. *Finally Darren painted a series of extreme highlights using Skull White – note the occasional flecks along the sides of the blade too.*

Red Armour and Blood Vial

The Sanguinor's deep red shoulder pads and the blood-filled vial that hangs from his waist provide ideal opportunities for a painter to bring in areas of contrasting colour to the miniature. Both of these reds are painted in a subty different way; after all, one is an armour plate and the other is a vial filled with blood.

Red Armour

Step 1. First, Darren basecoated the shoulder pad with a 1:1 mix of Mechrite Red and Scab Red – note how a fine line of black was left between the red and gold of the shoulder pad.

Step 2. The edges of the shoulder pad were shaded using a 1:1 mix of Scab Red and Chaos Black. By keeping this watered down Darren was able to blend it into the lighter red.

Step 3. Next, the shoulder pad was highlighted with a 1:1 mix of Mechrite Red and Blood Red.

Step 4. Darren then added a further highlight, this time using a 1:1 mix of Blood Red and Blazing Orange.

Step 5. The shoulder pad was highlighted using a 1:1 mix of Blazing Orange and Skull White.

Step 6. Finally, spots of pure Skull White were applied where the reflection of light would be most intense.

Vial

Step 1. Darren painted the top of the vial with a 1:1 mix of Codex Grey and Regal Blue. The blood was painted with Scab Red.

Step 2. Next the vial was shaded using a 1:1 mix of Chaos Black and Regal Blue. This included adding several dark reflective lines that run from top to bottom.

Step 3. The top part of the vial was highlighted with Fortress Grey, while the blood was highlighted with a 1:1:1 mix of Scab Red, Blood Red and Warlock Purple.

Step 4. The top of the vial was highlighted with Space Wolves Grey, the bottom with a 1:1 mix of Blood Red and Warlock Purple.

Step 5. Darren painted a fine line of Chaos Black through the centre of the dark reflective lines on the vial.

Step 6. For the last stage, Darren added some extreme highlights with Skull White, painting them alongside the dark reflective lines.

The Finished Miniature

Here you can see the completed Sanguinor miniature. When you look at the miniature as a whole, it is clear that Darren has used the same colours and painting techniques demonstrated across the whole miniature, for example the Sanguinor's iron halo and the chain around his neck were painted in the same way as the chalice. Likewise, the wings on the Blood Angels symbol at his waist and on his shoulder pad, were painted in exactly the same way as those on his back. The overall effect is one of a fabulously detailed miniature with a consistent colour palette.

We've shown the Sanguinor at slightly larger than actual size, so you can get a good look at the details on the finished model.

'EAVY METAL™ SHOWCASE

Lemartes, Guardian of the Lost

Mephiston, Lord of Death

Astorath the Grim

CITADEL Colour Chart

Citadel's range of paints, metallics, washes and varnish provides you with a comprehensive palette to paint your miniatures in any colour scheme or tone you wish. Foundation paints provide the perfect basecoat, Citadel Washes are fantastic for shading, while the Citadel Colour range contains great acrylic paints, specially formulated for a host of miniature-painting techniques.

Citadel Colour

- Sunburst Yellow
- Golden Yellow
- Blazing Orange
- Blood Red
- Red Gore
- Scab Red
- Dark Flesh
- Dwarf Flesh
- Elf Flesh
- Warlock Purple
- Liche Purple
- Regal Blue
- Ultramarines Blue
- Enchanted Blue
- Shadow Grey
- Space Wolves Grey
- Ice Blue
- Hawk Turquoise
- Dark Angels Green
- Snot Green

- Goblin Green
- Scorpion Green
- Rotting Flesh
- Camo Green
- Catachan Green
- Graveyard Earth
- Scorched Brown
- Bestial Brown
- Vermin Brown
- Snakebite Leather
- Bubonic Brown
- Vomit Brown
- Desert Yellow
- Kommando Khaki
- Bleached Bone
- Fortress Grey
- Codex Grey
- Chaos Black
- Skull White

Metallic Colour

- Burnished Gold
- Shining Gold
- Dwarf Bronze
- Tin Bitz
- Boltgun Metal
- Chainmail
- Mithril Silver

Citadel Wash

- Baal Red
- Asurmen Blue
- Leviathan Purple
- Devlan Mud
- Ogryn Flesh
- Gryphonne Sepia
- Thraka Green
- Badab Black

Citadel Varnish

- Gloss Varnish

Citadel Foundation

- Iyanden Darksun
- Macharius Solar Orange
- Mechrite Red
- Tausept Ochre
- Calthan Brown
- Khemri Brown
- Tallarn Flesh
- Dheneb Stone
- Gretchin Green
- Knarloc Green
- Orkhide Shade
- Fenris Grey
- Hormagaunt Purple
- Mordian Blue
- Charadon Granite
- Necron Abyss
- Adeptus Battlegrey
- Astronomican Grey